QUESTIONING

Teachers ask hundreds of questions every week, some requiring single word answers, others involving much more complex thought and understanding, many to do with the management of the class. Whole lessons can be built around one or two thought-provoking questions, involving the imagination, inviting children to recall vital information, understand a new concept, analyse, speculate and reason.

This workbook explains clearly the different types and patterns of questions teachers may ask and offers a wide range of useful practical exercises to enable both experienced and trainee teachers to improve their own and their colleagues' questioning skills.

George Brown is a former lecturer in Education at the University of Nottingham. He has written many books, including *Effective Teaching in Higher Education* (Routledge 1988) and, also with Ted Wragg, *Explaining* in the Leverhulme Primary Project *Classroom Skills* series.

Ted Wragg is head of the School of Education at Exeter University and the author of many books including *Class Management* and, again with George Brown, *Explaining* in this series. He writes a regular column in the *Times Educational Supplement* and is a frequent commentator for radio and television on educational matters.

Clive Carré is coordinator of the Leverhulme Primary Project and series editor for the *Classroom Skills* series. He has taught science at primary and secondary levels and has written and acted as a consultant on science materials in the UK, Australia and Canada.

LEVERHULME PRIMARY PROJECT

The Leverhulme Primary Project, based at Exeter University, directed by Ted Wragg and Neville Bennett and coordinated by Clive Carré is a major survey of primary teacher education since 1988. Its bank of valuable information about what actually happens in classrooms and how teachers are reacting to current changes in education will be used for a variety of publications including the *Classroom Skills* series.

LEVERHULME PRIMARY PROJECT ■ *Classroom Skills series*

All primary teachers need to master certain basic pedagogical skills. This set of innovative yet practical resource books for teachers covers each of those skills in turn. Each book contains

- Practical, written and oral activities for individual and group use at all stages of professional development
- Transcripts of classroom conversation and teacher feedback and photographs of classroom practice to stimulate discussion
- Succinct and practical explanatory text

Other titles in the series

TALKING AND LEARNING IN GROUPS	*Elisabeth Dunne and Neville Bennett*
CLASS MANAGEMENT	*E.C. Wragg*
EXPLAINING	*E.C. Wragg and George Brown*
EFFECTIVE TEACHING	*E.C. Wragg*

Leverhulme Primary Project ■ **Classroom Skills Series**

Series editor
Clive Carré

QUESTIONING

George Brown and E.C. Wragg

London and New York

First published 1993
by Routledge
11 New Fetter Lane, London EC4P 4EE

Simultaneously published in the USA and Canada
by Routledge
29 West 35th Street, New York, NY 10001

© 1993 E.C. Wragg and George Brown
Filmset in Palatino by
Selwood Systems, Midsomer Norton
Printed and bound in Great Britain by
Butler & Tanner Ltd, Frome and London

British Library Cataloguing in Publication Data

A catalogue record for this title is available from the British
Library.

Library of Congress Cataloging in Publication Data

Brown, George, 1935–
    Questioning/George Brown and E. C. Wragg.
        p.   cm.—(Leverhulme primary project classroom
skills series)
    Includes bibliographical references.
    ISBN 0–415–08386–9
    1. Questioning.   I. Wragg, E. C. (Edward
Conrad)   II. Title.   III. Series.
LB1027.44.B76   1993   92–24784
    372.13—dc20   CIP

For Emma
May her teachers teach her to ask the right questions – and how to tackle them.

CONTENTS

PREFACE

Improving the quality of what happens in primary school and preparing children for life in the twenty-first century requires the highest quality of professional training. The Leverhulme Primary Project *Classroom Skills* series and its companion series *Curriculum in Primary Practice* are designed to assist in this training.

The Leverhulme Primary Project *Classroom Skills* series focuses on the essential classroom competences. It explores the classroom strategies available to teachers and the patterns of classroom organization which best assist pupil learning. Throughout, it demonstrates that at the very heart of teacher education is the ability to make sense of what is going on in the classroom. This series of books is based on the research of the Leverhulme Primary Project, a three-year programme of research into various aspects of primary teacher education, funded by the Leverhulme Trust and carried out at the University of Exeter. The companion series, *Curriculum in Primary Practice* helps teachers to make judgements and devise strategies for teaching particular subjects.

Both series are designed to assist teachers at all stages of their professional development. They will be useful for:

- practising teachers
- student teachers
- college and university tutors
- school-based in-service coordinators
- advisory teachers
- school mentors and headteachers.

This book can be used as part of initial training or in in-service programmes in school. The text can also be read by individuals as a source of ideas and it will be helpful in teacher appraisal as an aid to developing professional awareness both for those being appraised and for the appraisers. Like all the books in both series, *Questioning* contains suggested activities which have been tried out by teachers and those in pre-service training and revised in the light of their comments.

We hope that both series will provoke discussion, help you to reflect on your current practice and encourage you to ask questions about everyday classroom events.

Clive Carré
University of Exeter

ACKNOWLEDGEMENTS

We wish to thank Neville Hatton of the University of Sydney for his suggestions and comments on this book, Jill Christie and Caroline Wragg who conducted much of the research on questioning as part of the Leverhulme Project, Mary Hamilton, Jo Fisher and many other teachers in local primary schools for their comments and suggestions and the activities. Last but not least we thank Trina Medlicott for her skills, speed, efficiency and patience in creating this book from the manuscript and tape recordings.

WHO AND WHAT IS THIS BOOK FOR?

This book has been written to help young and experienced teachers in service in primary schools to:

(a) reflect upon their uses of questions;

(b) develop their approaches to preparing, using and evaluating their own questions;

(c) explore ways in which pupils may be encouraged to question and to provide answers.

The book is not about how to teach the National Curriculum of England and Wales, although some examples of science, mathematics, English and other subjects are drawn from it. Nor is it concerned with getting children to respond like automata to tests. It is about persuading children to talk sensibly and to think about and to enjoy these processes. The primary focus of the book is upon everyday questions and questioning within the classroom, whether that classroom is organized in groups, for individualized learning or for whole class activities.

The book is partly based on studies of questioning conducted in the Leverhulme Primary Project. In one study a sample of twenty teachers was interviewed before and after they had taught two lessons. Ten of the teachers were working with children aged seven to nine and the remaining ten were working with younger children or with upper primary school classes. The researcher observed and recorded their lessons on audio tape and produced transcripts of the lessons, which were subsequently analysed in the light of the discussions with the teachers and pupils. In another study, more than 1000 questions asked by teachers were analysed.

The Leverhulme study of questioning provided the basis for some of this text, but other transcripts and studies were also used. The transcripts were provided by teachers and researchers working with younger and older children, so that readers can see and use ideas drawn from the whole range of the primary school. Details of the studies used in the text are given in the annotated bibliography and the references. Some of these studies were conducted in Australia and North America, all were concerned with deepening understanding of the processes of questioning. Readers might like to consult in particular the volume *Explaining* (Wragg and Brown 1993) in this series. There is much in common between the two notions – teachers seeking to explain often make use of questions.

This book is divided into six Units. As befits a text on questioning, each Unit addresses a key question. Within each Unit are summaries of relevant research, activities and tasks to try out on one's own or with colleagues or pupils. There are also various guidelines and suggestions on questioning. Unit 1 begins with the fundamental question: Why do we ask questions? It then considers the related questions: Why do teachers ask questions? and: Why do pupils ask questions? Unit 2 is concerned with what kind of questions are asked in the classroom and how they might usefully be classified. The tactics of questioning are the focus of Unit 3, and types of lessons (units of learning in modern parlance) are the focus of Unit 4. Unit 5 suggests ways of exploring how pupils learn and Unit 6 provides a framework for exploring approaches to preparing questions and lessons. An annotated bibliography and a list of references are provided. The Appendix offers some suggestions for running workshops.

The book may be used in at least four ways. First, you may simply read it. This will take most people no more than one evening. It will be time well spent because you will refresh your knowledge of questioning, you may be reminded of strategies and tactics that you know but forget to use, and you may be introduced to some new approaches and findings. Second, you can read the book and try out some of the activities with colleagues and pupils. This will provide you with practice, reflection and perhaps discussion of the issues involved, thereby deepening your understanding and developing your expertise on questioning. You may find that audio-recordings of lessons are a useful adjunct to the text. If you do use the text in this way, then try each suggested activity with pupils and colleagues at least twice. The first try is for you to learn what to do, the second is to enable you to help your colleagues and pupils to do them better. Comenius's adage is relevant here: 'Docemur docendo' – 'we learn as we teach'.

The third way is to use parts of the text as a basis for short in-service courses within the school. The notes and comments as well as the activities are of value for this purpose. You may also find helpful the suggestions for organizing a half-day course on questioning that are given in the Appendix. Used in this way you will learn from your colleagues' reports on their teaching and from discussing with them their approaches to the task. The fourth way is to use the text as the basis of an organized systematic course on the use of questions with primary school pupils. Such a course would take about five days (40 hours) and it is best tackled in blocks of time distributed through a couple of terms. This approach gives participants time to learn new approaches, to reflect on them, to use them in their teaching, to evaluate them and to bring back to the course their views, experiences and problems.

The following symbols are used throughout the book to denote:

 quotations from published material

 activities

transcripts of children or teachers talking and feedback from teachers

WHY DO WE ASK QUESTIONS?

It is rare to demand of people ... how do you spell rhododendron unless you really do not know the answer. Cross questioning, checking up and interrogation are rude in every day life, but the staple of classroom life.

Delamont 1984

A five-year-old girl returned from her first day at school and announced that her teacher was no good because she didn't know anything. When asked why she thought that, she replied that the teacher just kept on asking us things ...

 ACTIVITY 1

As a preliminary to reading the following Unit, please tackle one or more of the following activities.

1 Spend a few minutes jotting down your answers to the question 'Why do people ask questions?' Compare your notes with those of a few colleagues.

2 Spend a few minutes jotting down your answer to the question 'Why do teachers ask questions?' Compare your notes with those of a few colleagues.

3 Spend a few minutes jotting down your answers to the question 'Why do pupils ask questions?' Compare your notes with those of a few colleagues.

(Minimum time for this set of activities is about 45 minutes)

WHY DO PEOPLE ASK QUESTIONS?

The implication behind this child's remark was that we ask questions when we want to know something and, if you know the answer, then you don't need to ask. Broadly speaking, we can distinguish cognitive, affective and social reasons for asking questions in conversations, dealing with knowledge, feelings and relationships. We seek information or the solution to problems, we want to satisfy our curiosity or allay anxiety, we want to make contact with or deepen our understanding of another person. There are other reasons that may be subsumed under these three categories. You may already have thought of these when tackling Activity 1.

WHY DO TEACHERS ASK QUESTIONS?

Our reasons for asking questions of children are rather different from those in everyday conversation. Put another way, the rules of talk in the classroom are different from those in other contexts. We often ask questions of children, not to obtain new knowledge for ourselves but to find out what children already know. The principle is expressed in more precise language by Ausubel (1978):

 The most important single factor influencing learning is what the learner already knows. Ascertain this and teach him/her accordingly.

Other cognitive, and cognate, reasons for asking questions are to stimulate recall, to deepen understanding, to develop imagination and to encourage problem solving. Turney *et al.*, (1973) in their first edition of the Sydney Micro Series list twelve possible functions of questions (see Fig. 1.1). In addition to the functions that they list, questions

Why do we ask questions?

Figure 1.1 Some reasons for asking questions

- To arouse interest and curiosity concerning a topic.
- To focus attention on a particular issue or concept.
- To develop an active approach to learning.
- To stimulate pupils to ask questions of themselves and others.
- To structure a task in such a way that learning will be maximized.
- To diagnose specific difficulties inhibiting pupil learning.
- To communicate to the group that involvement in the lesson is expected, and that overt participation by all members of the group is valued.
- To provide an opportunity for pupils to assimilate and reflect upon information.
- To involve pupils in using an inferred cognitive operation on the assumption that this will assist in developing thinking skills.
- To develop reflection and comment by pupils on the responses of other members of the group, both pupils and teachers.
- To afford an opportunity for pupils to learn vicariously through discussion.
- To express a genuine interest in the ideas and feelings of the pupil.

Source: Turney *et al.* 1973

have other functions such as assisting classroom management and control (Mehan 1978).

Turney's list is rather more comprehensive than that of most young teachers who are, for the first time, considering the way they ask questions of pupils. For example, in a study of 190 teachers in US elementary schools (primary schools), Pate and Bremer (1967) asked teachers to provide reasons for asking questions. They found that 69 per cent of the statements emphasized questions to check knowledge and understanding, 54 per cent were concerned with diagnosing pupils' difficulties, 47 per cent stressed recall of facts and only 10 per cent stressed the use of questions to encourage pupils to think. Significantly, there were no responses that suggested that questions may be used to help pupils to learn from each other (see Dunne and Bennett 1990) or that questions may be used to encourage pupils themselves to ask questions.

During the past twenty years there has been a shift in understanding and valuing of the use of questions in classrooms. In Britain, this shift has been helped by the writings of Barnes (1969, 1976) and by various Government-commissioned reports: for example, the Cox Report (1989). The essence of the suggestions of these writings is that we need to consider the purposes of questions as well as the practice of questioning to encourage pupils to talk and think.

WHY DO TEACHERS ASK SPECIFIC QUESTIONS?

As well as asking oneself why do I ask questions in teaching, it is also instructive to ask oneself why am I asking this specific question and indeed, why am

medium ability classes reported more Checking (CH) questions and Revision (R) questions, whereas teachers of low ability classes tended to stress Understanding (U) and Management (M). Teachers of mixed ability classes tended to stress Understanding, Gaining Attention to move towards teaching point, Management and Revision.

Figure 1.2 is a classification of the reasons given by the teachers. If a teacher said 'To check understanding and knowledge', it was assigned to CH. It does not follow that a teacher's statement is exclusive of other categories, or that the reasons the teacher gave are the only reasons.

Among the secondary English teachers in the sample, the most common reasons given were gaining attention and management, whereas for the mathematicians and scientists the most common reasons were checking understanding and encouraging thought. The practical arts and second language teachers gave more revision and checking reasons, whereas history and geography teachers provided more encouraging understanding and gaining attention. On the basis of this small sample, the evidence suggested that teachers' reasons for asking questions, not surprisingly, vary according

Figure 1.2   Teachers' reasons for asking specific questions

		%
U	Encouraging thought, understanding of ideas, phenomena, procedures and values	33
CH	Checking understanding, knowledge and skills	30
G	Gaining attention to task. To enable teacher to move towards teaching point in the hope of eliciting a specific and obscure point, as a warm-up activity for pupils	28
R	Review, revision, recall, reinforcement of recently learnt point, reminder of earlier procedures	23
M	Management, settling down, to stop calling out by pupils, to direct attention to teacher or text, to warn of precautions	20
T	Specifically to teach whole class through pupil answers	10
J	To give everyone a chance to answer	10
BP	Ask bright pupils to encourage others	4
D	To draw in shyer pupils	4
PR	Probe children's knowledge after critical answers, redirect question to pupils who asked or to other pupils	3
O	To allow expressions of feelings, views and empathy	3
Q	Unclassifiable, unreadable, incoherent	2

I asking this specific question of this pupil. We asked these questions of a sample of forty teachers (Brown and Edmondson 1984) in English secondary schools. The results and classified system are shown in Figure. 1.2. In effect the system is a summary of the reasons given by the teachers; it is not a set of mutually exclusive categories. The most common reasons were: encouraging thought, checking understanding, gaining attention, revision and management.

The teachers who provided samples of questions from high ability classes used G (Gaining Attention) and U (Understanding) most frequently. Teachers of

to the subject or topic being taught, the class and its ability.

In one of the studies of questions in the primary school in the Leverhulme Primary Project, we asked teachers to identify three key questions and to discuss why they had chosen them. The teachers who had taught the most stimulating lessons very often provided a reason which contained a sense of looking ahead – the intention was evident. The least effective seemed to be looking nowhere or focused almost entirely upon what the children knew already. Perhaps most important of all, in the successful lessons, the key questions were related to the expressed aims of the lesson and provided the episodes of questioning and explaining during the lesson.

Another of the studies in the Leverhulme Primary Project involved recording more than 1000 questions asked by teachers in different primary classes. The questions asked were divided into three categories: *managerial* if they were to do with the running of the lesson (e.g. 'Have you got your books?'), *information/data* if they involved the recall of information (e.g. 'How many legs does an insect have?'), and *higher order* if pupils had to do more than just remember facts, for example, if they had to analyse, make generalizations or infer (e.g. 'Why is a bird not an insect?'). Here are some of the distributions obtained, given in percentages:

Whole class	22	Managerial	57
Small groups	12	Information/	
Individuals	66	data	35
		Higher order	8
TOTAL	100	TOTAL	100

There is no strong research evidence that one form of question is invariably better than another, but what observations would you make about the distributions given above? Suppose this were the distribution in your own lessons, would you want to make changes? If so, of what kind and why? And how would you achieve them?

We also analysed the distribution of questions in both categories combined, in order to see what types of questions were asked in what context. Here are the results, in descending order of frequency, so that the most common occurrence was managerial questions to individuals (37 per cent), and the least common was higher order questions to small groups (1 per cent):

managerial to individuals	37
information/data to individuals	24
managerial to whole class	12
information/data to whole class	8
managerial to small groups	8
higher order to individuals	5
information/data to small groups	3
higher order to whole class	2
higher order to small groups	1
TOTAL	100

Suppose a teacher decided that she was spending too much time asking managerial questions of individuals and would like to invest more effort in asking them to think more deeply about the subject matter of what they were learning, how might she set about this? Think in particular about class management (see the companion book to this, *Class Management*, Wragg 1993), and how children might become more independent.

WHY DO PUPILS ASK QUESTIONS?

Children may ask a lot of questions – but not usually in school. Indeed, one researcher estimated that in elementary schools in the United States most teachers ask questions at the rate of two a minute and most classes of pupils at the rate of two per hour (Susskind 1969 and 1979). In one Leverhulme study of questioning in the twenty lessons studied there were fewer than twenty questions by pupils and most of these questions were not concerned with thinking.

Most types of questions asked by primary school pupils of their teachers are procedural, such as 'What time are we going home?', 'Should we put the date?', rather than cognitive, such as 'Why is the sky blue?', or 'What happens if . . .?' The questions asked by primary school pupils of each other are often conversational rather than cognitive, to do with knowledge unless their teacher encourages them to ask questions. Torrance (1970) demonstrated how teachers can encourage nursery and infant children to ask better, thoughtful questions. Her studies indicated that young children working in groups of four to six tended to ask more and better questions than did children working individually or in groups of twelve to thirty. They asked more questions and more penetrating, hypothesis and information seeking questions when given objects to manipulate or materials to experiment with than when only shown objects and asked to watch them being demonstrated. They displayed more interest and thought when asked puzzling questions. For example, when looking at a picture a teacher asked 'Why does some of the grass look green and some blue? Why didn't they cut all of the grass?' This resulted in a great deal of discussion and explanation. The least effective method of getting children to volunteer questions and observations appeared to be the excessive use of naming questions, such as 'What do they call this?' 'What colour is the grass?'

Torrance's findings and those of earlier and subsequent writers indicate strongly the

Why do pupils ask questions?

importance of *practical experience* and questioning. Piaget's well-known adage (Piaget and Inhelder, 1969) that: 'All logical thinking arises out of the manipulation of objects' could well be extended to 'and the asking of questions'.

There are, of course, reasons other than cognitive or procedural that dispose children to ask questions. Most salient of these reasons is probably attention-seeking and so we may have to explore the reasons underlying the attention-seeking of a particular pupil and develop appropriate relationships and strategies to help that pupil – always bearing in mind the needs of other pupils.

PURPOSES AND REASONS

The underlying purpose and reason for asking questions are both simple and complex. Put simply, questions are asked to facilitate learning, so they are linked to the aims of lessons and the underlying purpose of the lesson. The complexity increases as we unfold the purposes and we become aware of myriads of reasons for asking questions and for asking specific questions of specific pupils. The reasons may be classified in terms of types – cognitive (knowledge and understanding), affective (to do with the emotions), social, procedural – or in terms of immediate short-term and long-term goals. As well as asking questions of pupils, we do ask ourselves questions implicitly and, preferably, explicitly when we are preparing lessons or topics and when we are evaluating our own performance as teachers. Key questions should be linked to our aims, for in so doing they provide structures for us as well as for pupils. They also provide us with lessons within lessons. Finally, there is the question why did we ask the question 'Why do teachers ask questions?'

 ACTIVITY 2

1 Look back at your answers to the three questions given in Activity 1. Add any points that you have discovered or rediscovered in this Unit.
2 Why do pupils ask so few questions? List the possible reasons and choose the most important reasons. Compare your choices with those of a few colleagues.
  What implications do these reasons have for organizing your classroom and your teaching?
3 Teach a brief lesson on the topic 'Why do people ask questions?'

If you are teaching younger children you may wish to do it through a story. Alternatively you may ask them to each provide some questions about an object or procedure or a set of objects and then list the sorts of questions that they asked. If you are working with older children, you might ask them to list the kinds of questions that one could ask about an object or to produce a picture that illustrates this. (A useful topic for this activity is purchasing a new car or buying someone a present.) You might also ask them to develop a set of 'what', 'how' and 'why' questions about an object. With upper classes of the primary school, you might invite them to offer reasons why teachers and pupils ask questions.

4 Read the following transcript and note and highlight your answers to these questions:
  i)   Identify some managerial questions.
  ii) Identify the first key question of the lesson.
  iii) Are all managerial questions really questions? Or are some really commands?
  iv) Why did you think the teacher asked the key question?
  v)   Was the next sequence of the lesson appropriate?
  vi) How would you have changed this sequence and lesson?
  vii) Why did we choose this transcript?

 Transcript 1.1

T: Right! Can you all sit down please and make a start. I'm sorry about the delay but I think we're all together now. Can I have you all looking this way. Put everything down. Can you remember back to the end of last half term we did some work together on some creative writing with the title 'Spring' and today a small group of us will develop that work ... I want you to listen to the music and if you want to close your eyes you can if it helps you to concentrate, and just allow the music to bring up into your mind lots of ideas, lots of images. Now perhaps before we actually listen to the music I wonder if we could predict what this music will be like. The subject is going to be Spring, let's write that up. I don't think you've heard this before, I haven't played it to you anyway. What do you imagine the music might be like? Claire?
P: Bouncy?
T: Right, bouncy music, OK, any other words? Fast?, anybody else? Why did you suggest those two words for example?
P: Because of bouncing lambs in meadows

T: Right, lambs bouncing around, springy yes! When we think of Spring as the season, what immediately comes into your mind first of all?

P: Flowers.

T: Flowers, good.

P: Sun.

T: Sun!

P: Animals.

T: Animals – what sort of animals?

P: Sheep.

T: Sheep, birds in the air?

P: New animals!

T: Right! New born baby animals because what festival is there at Springtime?

P: Easter.

T: Right! Easter and Easter is a time of what?

P: Joy and sorrow . . .

T: To begin with what I would like you to do is just listen to it remember it's about Spring, it's the beginning of life.

At the beginning of the music I want you to remember you're coming out of Winter, you're coming out of darkness, you're coming out of deadness if you like, into new life, sounds of the flute, birds' delight, day and night, nightingale in the dale, gale in the dale, lark in skies merrily, merrily. Little boy full of joy, little girl small and sweet, pop does crow, so do you, merry voice, infant noise, very merrily do we come to school, little lamb here I am, piping down the valley wild piping songs of pleasant dreams, piper sit thee down and write a book that all may read and then you vanished from my sight and I plucked a hollow reed and I made a rural pen and I stained the water clear!

Now while the music's playing I just want you to think back on all the images that the music is bringing to mind. What I am going to do in a moment or two is give out large sheets of paper and in the groups where you are, rather like before, I want you to write down, you can talk together among yourselves, perhaps one person can write down the suggestions and the others can talk about it, all the different musical images that this music on Spring conjures up . . .

Right! I'll start the music . . .

5 Prepare and teach a brief lesson to your class, audio-record the lesson and save it for subsequent analysis. Before reading the next unit, listen to the tape and make notes on it.

WHAT KINDS OF QUESTIONS DO WE ASK?

I keep six honest serving men (They taught me all I knew); Their names are What and Why and When, And How and Where and Who.

Rudyard Kipling,

I keep six honest serving men

In this unit we explore the kinds of questions that teachers ask their pupils and how those questions may be classified. We then offer some activities and suggestions to help you to reflect upon approaches to questioning, including your own.

STUDIES OF QUESTIONING

If you have been teaching in a primary school for the past six years then you probably have asked half a million questions in your classes. This rather startling finding has proved remarkably stable this century. Stevens (1912) reported that teachers appeared to ask 400 questions per day, that 65 per cent of those questions were concerned with recall of textbook information; that learning consisted mostly of responding to teacher questions and there were virtually no questions asked by pupils that were concerned directly with learning. Twenty-three years later Haynes (1935) discovered that 12–13 year olds were asked by their teachers 70 per cent of questions requiring factual answers and only 17 per cent that fostered pupils' thinking. In his 1970 review of teachers' questions, Gall noted that 60 per cent of teacher questions required pupils to recall facts in much the same way as that in which they were presented, and only 20 per cent required pupils to think beyond a level of recall; the remaining 20 per cent involved procedural matters such as classroom management. Other writers (e.g. Stodolsky *et al*. 1981) provide similar but slightly

different percentages and Galton, Simon and Kroll (1980) in their study of primary and middle schools report that only 12 per cent of teaching time was devoted to questions: of this 29 per cent was devoted to factual questions, 23 per cent to ideas, and more than 47 per cent to tasks of provision and routine management. It does seem that teachers ask several factual questions – and pupils spend much of their time answering them.

The evidence on frequency of questions is not a good guide to pupil achievement. Correlations between question frequency and achievement are weak. Indeed, one writer (Dillon 1981) argues that excessive questioning makes pupils dependent and passive. Too much questioning can evoke anxiety and too little may mute thought. There is division of opinion in the research literature about the extent to which types of questions asked are related to pupil achievement. Higher order (thought) questions do promote thinking and lower order (factual) questions do promote recalled facts. The only conclusion that can be drawn from this is that you have to choose what kinds of learning you want to promote and then choose appropriate types of questions. This conclusion is particularly important in primary education, where teachers face the challenging task of laying the foundations of understanding in science, mathematics and the arts.

Barnes and Todd (1977) showed that pupils who worked in small discussion groups, without the teacher present, generated more exploratory questions, hypotheses and explanations than when teachers were present. Using slightly different perspectives, Edwards and Furlong (1978) described their investigations of traditional classrooms in terms of the teacher's authority and control of knowledge. The teacher provided a framework into which pupil talk is fitted and that talk is assessed according to the closeness of fit.

It seems to us that these findings show how important discussion and free play of language are for developing understanding. One strategy to use in this respect is to explore the patterns of thinking of pupils in their own terms and then to show links with the language and assumptions of a subject.

TYPES OF QUESTIONS

Broadly speaking the content of questions may be categorized as predominantly *conceptual*, predominantly *empirical* and predominantly *value-related*. Conceptual questions are concerned with ideas, definitions and reasoning. Empirical questions require answers based upon facts or upon experimental findings. Value questions are concerned with relative worth and merit, with moral and environmental issues. These broad categories of the content of questions often overlap and they are by no means clear-cut. Some questions, particularly key questions, involve elements of all three types of questions.

This classification of questions may seem, at first sight, remote from teaching young children and more akin to work in universities. Yet, given the importance of laying foundations in the sciences and arts, it follows that these questions are likely to be found, in some form or other, in classes in the primary school at all levels from reception class to upper junior school classes. As well as types of questions, there are dimensions of questioning. These are discussed in the next section.

Conceptual questions

Here is an example of a conceptual topic. In sorting and counting exercises, it is not unusual to ask pupils in a reception class to sort wooden beads into piles of different colours such as brown and blue. If the pupils are asked 'Are there more brown beads than blue beads?' then most young pupils can answer the question. If the question is posed 'Are there more wooden beads than blue beads?' then some pupils cannot work out the correct answer, others do work out the correct answer and a few think the question is so obvious that it is trivial. The pupils who provide the correct answers have managed, in this context, to apply set theory or logic to solve the reasoning problem. The answer might have been arrived at empirically by counting the number of wooden beads and then the number of

blue beads, but even then a logical connection between the two findings has to be made.

Empirical questions

Empirical types of questions involve observation, recall of facts and possible experimentation. If reasoning is used, it is to confirm the facts or to show the connections between the facts and observations. Here are a couple of examples drawn from the transcripts we collected in the Leverhulme study. Both are from science lessons with 7–8 year olds.

✳ Transcript 2.1

T:	When I blew up the balloon, Sarah said that the air presses against the side of the cup and lifts the cup up with the balloon. So what do you think is going to happen if I let go of the cup?
Claire:	It's going to stay.
T:	It's going to stay with the balloon. What if I start to let go of the balloon?
Claire:	It will fall off.
Jonathan:	All the air will start coming out and friction on the side of the cup will start letting go, so then the friction will stop and then it will fall off.
T:	Gosh! we've got another word in here – friction! – say it again, really loud this time.
Jonathan:	Well, when the air goes out the friction will kind of come off the cup and then the friction will let go of the cup and then the cup will drop off.
T:	Right! So Jonathan is saying that there is some friction holding the balloon and the cup and that when the air comes out of the balloon, the cup is going to drop, off – does anybody else think that the cup's going to drop off? Who's not sure, be honest, it doesn't matter what you think. So if I let go of it – the cup drops to the floor – right, OK, so you've got some cups in front of you and you've got four balloons, so you can try it. Now what have you got to do when you're doing it?
Claire:	Don't let the air out!
T:	Don't let the air out, keep it in, right. Let's have a look at Rebecca's because she's got her balloon up quite a long way.

Are there more wooden beads than blue beads?

Transcript 2.2

T: Yes! Super! OK. So, if we think about stables and barns and pigsties. What? OK, that's fine. If we think about those places that animals live in, why do you think they go inside? Why do you think they don't always live outside in a field?
P: In the winter they get cold.
T: Not just in the winter. What other times might they get cold, what about the time of day? – Nathan.
P: Autumn.
T: Well Autumn and Winter they get cold – Lee?
P: When the wind blows.
T: What about at night time – what do we do at night time?
P: Sleep.
T: And we get tucked up in a nice warm bed, so do you think they get tucked up in hay?

Value questions

Value questions are concerned with morals, social concerns such as poverty, health issues such as smoking, and environmental issues such as pollution. These types of questions are likely to arise in many subjects.

ACTIVITY 3

Value questions

This transcript is taken from an upper primary school class discussion in Sydney, New South Wales. Read through it and pick out a few questions concerned with values, ideas and facts.

✳ **Transcript 2.3**

T: We want to think particularly today of some of the problems of old people. Now of course we could equally talk about their happiness. Not all old people are sad, but because we want to talk about communities later on, we want to focus on their problems. I have put a poem on the board, it's only a fairly brief one. I want you to have a look at this poem and at the end of that I want you to tell me something about the problem of this man as represented in the poem. [uncovers poem written on blackboard] Perhaps someone would like to read it to us before we start to talk about it. Bruce would you like to?

P: If you go there just before it is dark,
If you go to the park, the wind blows and the leaves cling to the fences and the papers fly,
He sits there on the seat by the track an old, old man; A fag in his lips, brown teeth, white hair and a wet chin.

T: All right, now what about that man, what are some of the problems you think he might face? – Linda

P: He sounds as if he is very old.

T: Yes.

P: And he's got nothing left.

T: All right, that's a good answer.

P: I think that he's poor and he's just sitting in the park on a brisk day and he's remembering about his childhood.

T: Why do you say he's poor – what makes you have that impression?

P: Oh, just the whole poem just gives you the impression that he's poor.

T: All right, we'll put that up on the board in a moment – Stephen

P: And I think he is an old tramp because we find lots of them in our parks round the community.

T: Good.

P: And quite a few of these people don't shave and they drink methylated spirits and things like that.

T: All right, there are a lot of factors that you have told us, now why do you think people might drink methylated spirits? Why do they sit around in the park all day – James?

P: Because they haven't got a home or if they have it's not much of a home and it's too expensive to try to buy beer or whisky or anything like that, so it's pretty cheap to buy methylated spirits.

T: Good, we're coming back to this point up here aren't we? Somebody said that this man was poor and you are saying that they buy methylated spirits because beer is too dear. There's one word that I am thinking of, they lack lots of what?

P: Education.

T: Well, education is one thing that we can come to in a moment.

P: They might be lonely and they look at all the birds and things to pass the time.

T: All right, these are very good answers but there is one word that I want us to get up here [points to the space near word 'Poor']. There are lots of things that go together because they lack what? Lots of?

P: Money.

T: Money! Right! I'm thinking of ordinary old money . . .

P: They are probably very lonely and they go to the park and watch all the birds and just think back, and they think how lovely nature is and how the city is being destroyed and all that.

DIMENSIONS OF QUESTIONS

Given the range and frequency of questions that we ask of our pupils, it is curious that few of us attempt to classify the kind of questions we ask or indeed even to check occasionally how many questions we ask in lessons. As indicated earlier, there are several ways of classifying questions for the purpose of research. Here we want to concentrate on a broad classification of the dimensions of questions that people have found useful when reflecting upon the range and kind of questions that they ask of their pupils.

The narrow/broad dimension

Questions may be framed to require a relatively brief, specific answer (for example, What is the capital of Outer Mongolia?) or to require a relatively wide ranging example (for example, What did you do yesterday?). These questions may be represented as points on a dimension, although you should bear in mind that a narrow question in one context may be a broad question in another. The narrow/broad dimension is sometimes described as closed/open or convergent/divergent questions. Not surprisingly, excessive use of narrow questions yields short answers and frequently inhibits discussion. Sometimes the form of a broad question is used, yet the teacher is searching for a narrow specific answer. Such pseudo-broad questions can evoke frustration rather than information. In one study more than 50 per cent of this type of question failed to receive any answers from pupils, so the teacher answered his or her own question (Barnes 1969).

The observation/recall/thought dimension

This is perhaps the most difficult dimension to grasp. Recall and observation are intimately related in children. Put another way, you cannot observe or describe your observation without the use of recall of other things and ideas. However, the recall of facts can of course occur in the absence of observation. The recall of facts or previously known ideas influences observations and also provides the basis for thinking: hence, many teachers begin their lessons with a request for a recall or for observation. Broadly speaking, 'recall' questions test existing knowledge and observation, whereas 'thought' questions create new knowledge and ideas in the learner.

Recall questions are often used in the initial stages of a lesson to assess knowledge and to start the children thinking. However, a danger of this approach is that the pupils may be puzzled because the question seems too simple or, they may simply be bored and become disruptive.

As indicated earlier, our study of more than 1000 teachers' questions showed only eight per cent of these required higher order thinking, involving children in going beyond the mere recall of facts. There are several reasons for this, one particularly important reason being that teachers do not necessarily prepare such questions, but somehow expect them to arise spontaneously. It may be that if we want to ask questions which get children to think, then we've got to think ourselves about the questions we are going to ask them.

The dimension of 'recall/thought' is sometimes confused with the narrow/broad dimension. Yet it is clear that some questions may be narrow thought questions: for example, 'Are there more grandfathers in the world than fathers?' They may be narrow recall questions: for example, 'What date was the battle of Hastings?' Some may be broad recall questions: for example, 'What did you do yesterday?' and some may be broad thought questions: for example, 'How can unemployment be reduced in our society?' When higher order or thought questions are used they yield a greater number of responses from children, particularly when the higher order questions are broad. Such questions also yield greater gains in understanding

and more positive evaluations of teaching (Merlino 1977). However, we should bear in mind when using the recall/thought dimension that what may require a six-year-old to think may only require a nine-year-old to recall.

The confused/clear dimension

Clear questions are usually brief, direct and firmly anchored in the context of the lesson. Confusions are generated by questions embedded in a set of ancillary statements (or, even worse, in other questions) or when the context is not obvious. Some examples of common errors in questioning are given in Unit 3, on tactics.

The encouraging/threatening dimension

The same question may be asked in a variety of ways, which encourage or inhibit pupil responses. Given that we may want children to think and contribute to discussions, we should usually adopt encouraging modes of questioning and responding. This is not to say that questions should not confront or challenge, but the right turn of voice and phrase can turn a perceived threat into an acceptable challenge.

a ACTIVITY 4

Analysing your questions

Figure 2.1 sets out a simple system based upon the dimensions of questions that may be used to analyse your questions. Management and procedural questions are omitted in this analysis of your teaching. The system is easiest to use on a sample of the questions that you ask. First, write down a sample as you are listening to an audio-tape of your own lesson or someone else's, and then analyse the questions. The analysis may be carried out by two or three colleagues working together and then analysing and comparing their lessons. In using the system, do bear in mind the ages and abilities of the children that you are teaching. As indicated earlier, one child's thought may be another child's recall. Last but not least, don't expect to agree on the dimensions of every single question sampled.

Figure 2.1 **'Ask it'**. This system of analysis is designed to help you to classify the questions asked while teaching a class, group or individual. Simply note down a sample of the questions asked, from a tape-recording of a lesson, classify each question on each dimension and examine the pattern of questions asked.

QUESTIONS	DIMENSIONS								
	Recall	Observ.	Thought	Broad	Narr.	Confused	Clear	Encour.	Threatn.

You will find that this activity helps you to identify different kinds of questions. It helps you to become more aware of the questions that you ask and it can help you to improve your use of questions in class. Simply put a tick in any column whenever it seems appropriate. For example, the teacher may ask the question: 'Is the ball floating or sinking?' You might decide this is 'observation' because the child must look, 'narrow' because the answer is yes or no, 'clear', as it refers to a specific object the child can see before him, and neither 'encouraging' nor 'threatening', so you would leave that dimension blank. On the other hand, if the question were 'Why is the ball sinking?' some of your choices might be different, as more complex thought processes are involved and the child might need to know about 'buoyancy' and 'density'.

 ACTIVITY 5

1 Read the following transcripts and classify the questions using 'Ask it' (Figure 2.1) except for the encouraging/threatening dimension. Compare your analysis with those of colleagues, if possible. In so doing, look not only at the questions but the pattern, if any, in the sequence of questions asked.

 Transcript 2.4

The lesson was on the different features of fruit (6–7 year-olds).

T: Now, could you just pass me the fruits that are on the table, please. There are all sorts of fruits, actually this isn't what we would think of as a fruit but today we're going to call it a fruit, it's a tomato. Put your hand up if you know what that's called. Lots of you know the name of that – Donna, do you know?
P: No.
T: Emma – do you know?
P: Lemon.
T: A lemon.
P: A melon.
T: A lemon, what's Aaron getting muddled up with? He said melon. Does anybody know what a melon is, because it's a very different fruit?
P: A big fruit.
T: Yes it is a big fruit – what colour is it? – Sarah?
P: Yellow.
T: Yes it is yellow and it tastes very different to this, so a melon is a very different fruit – can you say lemon?
P: Lemon.
    (All together)
T: And melon – I haven't got a melon, I'm afraid. Can anybody tell me why it's like that – Christopher, what has happened to it?
P: Bruised.
T: It might well be bruised – anything else Gemma?

P: Gone off.
T: How do you know it's gone off?
P: There's all white stuff in the middle.
T: It's got white and blue on it – do we know what that's called?
P: A lemon.
T: No! the white and blue bits, Dean.
P: Duck.
T: Dirt?
P: No! Duck.
T: I am being silly here – why can't I understand what you're saying?
P: A duck.
T: A picture like there – it looks like a duck does it?

 Transcript 2.5

This lesson was on the question 'Why is it that birds can fly?' The extract is taken from the fourth minute into the lesson.

T: How big are your muscles David? Where are your muscles?
P: Here. [pointing]
P: Everywhere.
T: What are muscles for?
P: To make sure you can move.
T: How do they work?
P: If you don't have any muscles you'd just be flab and if you've got muscles then you can jump around and all that.
T: Very good, thank you very much John – now we've got a picture of it – find this muscle here and rest your hand on top of it. [puts hand on bicep]
P: Mine can go really high!
T: How do you make it go really high then John?
P: You've just got to flex it up and turn it round.
T: . . . so do you think bird muscles are actually bigger than that?
P: No.
T: I think they've got more muscles than us though.
P: Yes, because they're smaller and they can fit more in.
T: What do you think, Luke?
P: If you're bigger, then you might get a bit more than if you're smaller.
T: So if you've got more muscles if you are bigger – you'll have to think about that one and find out a bit more about it – Yes, Adam?
P: The humming bird is small, so he can go really fast and he's lighter.

Why is it that birds can fly?

T:　Do you think that that helps him fly – the fact that he's lighter?

P:　Yes . . .

2　Think of a topic that you are going to teach. Write down a sample of 10 questions that you might ask your pupils. Then classify them using the narrow/broad, recall/observation/thought and clear/confused dimensions. Exchange questions but not classifications with a colleague and classify each other's questions. Compare and discuss your classifications. Now consider if and how some of the questions could be improved. Discuss what sort of response you would expect each question to get from your class, and then teach your lesson. See what actual response you obtain, as well as how accurate you were about the impact of the questions.

WHAT ARE THE TACTICS OF EFFECTIVE QUESTIONING?

In his teaching the wise man guides his students but does not pull them along; he urges them to go forward and does not suppress them; he opens the way but does not take them to the place; ... if his students are encouraged to think for themselves we may call the man a good teacher.

(Confucius c. 500 BC)

Questions are only as good as the answers that they get. So it is important to consider not only the types of question that we ask but also the tactics of asking those questions.

One obvious tactic of effective questioning is to minimize our errors. So we begin this unit by inviting you to do Activity 6, which is based upon Figure 3.1. The notion of 'error' is a subjective one, so you might reflect on the extent to which you agree or disagree with the list below.

Figure 3.1 Some common errors in questioning

- Asking too many questions at once.
- Asking a question and answering it yourself.
- Asking questions only of the brightest or most likeable.
- Asking a difficult question too early.
- Asking irrelevant questions.
- Always asking the same types of questions.
- Asking questions in a threatening way.
- Not indicating a change in the type of question.
- Not using probing questions.
- Not giving pupils the time to think.
- Not correcting wrong answers.
- Ignoring answers.
- Failing to see the implications of answers.
- Failing to build on answers.

ACTIVITY 6

1 Put a tick by any of the 'errors' given in Figure 3.1 which you think you have committed within the last few weeks. If you do not tick any item then you do not need to read the rest of this section, but if you are honest ...

Compare your 'errors' with those of a few colleagues. Discuss how you might avoid committing those errors. What other errors in questioning do you have?

2 Teach and audio-record a segment of a lesson (or invite a colleague to observe a lesson and sample the questions that you use). Use the check-list of Fig. 3.1 to identify and discuss any 'errors', you may have made. Reflect with your colleague how the questioning might have been improved.

The Key Tactics

The key tactics in questioning are:
1 Structuring
2 Pitching and putting clearly
3 Directing and distributing
4 Pausing and pacing
5 Prompting and probing
6 Listening and responding
7 Sequencing

Structuring

Structuring consists of providing signposts for the sequence of questions and the topic. The structuring may be a brief exposition of the topic, a review, a series of questions and explanations based on a previous lesson or a statement of objectives.

Sometimes structuring moves are described as 'pre-formulators' (French and McClure 1983). Pre-formulators indicate the kinds of answers that the teacher expects. French and McClure use the term 'orientations' to describe direct appeals to pupils' experience. Again these are concerned with structuring. In cognitive psychology, Ausubel (1978) uses the term 'advance organizers' to describe the activation and direction of students' learning to what is going to be learnt. Whether we approach structuring from the standpoint of classroom language studies or from that of cognitive psychology, the important point is that structure with a well-defined focus is an essential tactic of effective questioning. We discuss more fully the use of 'advance organizers' (saying in effect, 'This is what we are going to do') in the companion book to this one, *Explaining* (Wragg and Brown 1993).

ACTIVITY 7

Examples of structuring

Two attempts at structuring are given in Transcripts 3.1 and 3.2. Neither is perfect. You might like to consider how they might be improved.

Transcript 3.1

T: Right children I just want you to watch what I do at the moment. I am just going to give you a little demonstration and so I want you to watch carefully. I hope it works. Right. Now when I let go of the cup and I am going to hold the balloon tight, what do you think is going to happen? Sarah says that the air presses against the side of the cup and lifts the cup up with the balloon. What do you think is going to happen if I let go of the cup? Claire?

Transcript 3.2

T: Now, as I was saying, when I give *you* **the clues**, you give *me* **thinking**, when it gets to the last two clues I am pretty sure that everybody will know. Right, here we go, Number 1. John are

you listening? Now the creature I am thinking of today, has the ability, is able, to make at least twelve different sounds, right. Now think about that and don't say anything to anybody. This animal likes to live in groups of up to twelve or more. Don't put your hand up, I don't need it. I want you to be thinking in there [points to head]. This creature is a peaceful animal. He doesn't have many enemies, his main enemy unfortunately is man. [Clues continue in this way].

'Pitching' and putting questions clearly – choosing your words

'Pitching' questions refers to selecting appropriately the recall/thought and narrow/broad dimensions described in Unit 2. All four types of questions – narrow-recall, broad-recall, narrow-thought and broad-thought – should be used when pitching questions. Sometimes it may be necessary to pitch a variety of broad-recall questions, at other times you may want to use a narrow-thought question. Of course, you should bear in mind that what may be a difficult thought question for one pupil or class of pupils may be obvious to another pupil or class of pupils.

Putting questions clearly involves using words and phrases that are appropriate to the group. A classic error made by newly qualified graduate student teachers in primary schools is to ask questions in the language of their degree subject:

'What do you think an ecological succession is?'

Such questions, particularly embedded in long rambling phrases, are likely to confuse and generate problems of class control. Sometimes the question may be put clearly by providing strong hints of the answer, for example:

'Was Mr Wilson, Mr Heath or Mrs Thatcher the Prime Minister for the longest time?'

The correct 'register' (that is, the appropriateness of the language used for the person addressed) is what is crucial. You might ask undergraduates:

'What is the etiology of dental caries?'

but a better choice of language for eight-year-olds would be:

'Why do sweets rot your teeth?'

Directing and distributing

Undirected questions often lead to chorus answers and lack of control. Hence the importance of directing questions by name, gesture, head movement or facial expression.

Distributing questions around the group not only involves more pupils but it also reduces the risk of losing attention and class control. Often we favour, unconsciously, asking bright or knowledgeable pupils, if only because their answers are more rewarding to us.

We can formalize the distribution – by asking every pupil in a small group in turn (something which teachers we interviewed during the Leverhulme research did not favour) – or we can distribute the questions randomly around the class. Certain parts of the room can get ignored by a beginning teacher. Children at the side of the classroom may be ignored when the teacher is in the centre at the front. The groups of pupils at the back may be ignored if a teacher is seated at a desk. It is worth considering where your blind spots are when distributing questions. In another volume in this series (*Class Management* by Ted Wragg) there is a fuller consideration of the tendency to address questions to children sitting in a V-shaped wedge in front of the teacher. Sometimes, in a discussion, a pupil may make a substantial point or provide an answer that requires further diagnosis and elaboration, so you may need to store that answer or contribution away or come back to it at a later point.

Part of the tactics of directing and distributing questions is monitoring the body language of the pupils. By looking at pupils you can often identify those who wish to contribute, those who are not attending and those who are puzzled. The point may seem obvious in a book; it is less obvious in the classrooms of newly qualified teachers.

Pausing and pacing

Student teachers often ask more questions than they receive answers to (Brown 1978). This failure is often due to lack of pauses, which in turn may be due to insecurity in the teacher role. The testimony of experienced teachers and the studies reviewed by Tobin (1987) show that pausing briefly after a question and after an answer encourages more pupils to answer, more of the pupils to provide longer answers and more questions from pupils. Some of these findings may be because teachers who use pauses also tend to use a wide variety of questions and vary the pace of questions. Pauses act as signals for pace. Drill questions can be asked quickly, whereas more complex questions require longer pauses. After all, if you want pupils to think before giving their answer, then you need to give them the time to think. As an aside, intriguing deep questions might sometimes be asked at the end of a lesson so that pupils have a long time to think – until the next lesson on that topic.

Prompting and probing

Prompts and probes are follow-up questions when the first answers are inadequate or inappropriate. Prompts contain hints, probes require more precise or detailed answers.

An example of prompting was given earlier in this section on structuring (see Activity 7). The answer was contained in the question. Three other forms of prompts are:

1 Rephrasing the question in different, perhaps simpler words that relate more to the pupil's knowledge and experience.
2 Asking simple questions that lead back to the original question.
3 Providing a review of information given and questions that will help the pupil to recall or see the answer.

Probing questions are probably the most important tactic for developing the thinking of pupils. There are several types of probing question: some examples are given in Figure 3.2.

Probing questions may be related to the encouraging/threatening dimension mentioned in Unit 2. If they are asked in an encouraging way, then they are providing a challenge and even fun. If asked in a threatening way, they can inhibit thinking and demotivate learning. Probing questions, if used insensitively, can lead to management problems. Intensive teacher questioning of one pupil can lead to pupil disruption, even if the line of questioning is gentle. Teasing out the full answer from one pupil may lead to the loss of interest of other members of the class.

Listening and responding

Our capacity to listen diminishes with anxiety, so it is not surprising that sometimes we do not listen carefully to the answers of pupils and so do not respond appropriately to their answers and comments. Four types of listening may be identified:

'Body language'

Skim listening. This is little more than awareness that a pupil is talking to you. Often you do this when the answers seem irrelevant, where you want to get on with what you are doing or are thinking of other matters.

Figure 3.2 Examples of probing questions

- Does that always apply?
- Can you give me an example of that?
- How does that fit in (relevance)?
- You say it is X, which particular kind of X?
- What are the exceptions?
- Why do you think that is true?
- Is there another view?
- What is the idea behind that?
- Can you tell me the difference between the two?

Note These examples may be modified in various ways. They are presented here only to give the flavour of the skill of probing and not to provide a mechanical checklist of all the different approaches to probing.

Survey listening Here you are trying to build a mental map of what the pupil is talking about. The listener filters out extraneous material and identifies the key points or misunderstandings of the pupil. This tactic is particularly important with young children. At its core is the capacity to understand how young children think and talk.

Search listening is active searching for specific information to an answer or a set of answers. Although it is important to search, it is also important not to overlook other answers or responses, for they may tell us more than our original question did.

Study listening is a subtle blend of search and survey listening, which goes beyond the words that the pupils use to their underlying meaning and uncertainties. It isn't possible to study listen all the time to one's pupils. What is more important is to be aware of the level of listening which you are currently using.

Responding

Responding is the move you make after a pupil answers or comments. Responding moves are, in a sense, the lynch pins of a lesson. They are important, therefore, in sequencing and structuring a lesson. They are the mechanisms whereby new information is introduced, the topic is changed, the discussion is moved on and the lesson is moved back on course. Responding moves are some of the most difficult tactics for newly qualified teachers to master. Figure 3.3 contains some of the more common responding moves.

Three important ways of conveying interest are:

1 To take a pupil's answer and build on it or invite other pupils to build on it – 'A spider's not an insect, that's right Caroline. Can anyone think why people believe it's an insect when it isn't really?'

2 To refer to a previous contribution from a pupil and to link it to the present contribution, thereby showing the connections between the pupil's own contributions and the topic under discussion – 'Now, Peter's told us that the magnet picked up the paperclip and Sally said it wouldn't pick up a brass curtain ring, so what does a magnet pick up?'

3 To incorporate the pupil's contributions (by name) into your summaries and reviews of what has been learnt in the lesson – 'So Jacky's guess was right. People who eat more sweets did have

Figure 3.3   Responding to answers and comments

Answer/Comment	*Teacher response*
ignored	asks someone else
	changes question
	changes topic
acknowledged	asks someone else
	changes question
	changes topic
repeated verbatim	merely states it
	inflects voice to convert into question
part of answer/comment echoed	merely states it
	inflects voice to convert into question
paraphrased	paraphrases directly
	expresses paraphrase in the form of a question
praise contribution	praises contribution
	praises contribution and elaborates
	praises contribution and uses it to build on explanation and question
corrected	corrects incorrect part of answer
	asks others to correct incorrect part of answer
prompted	asks prompting questions or supplies direct hint to pupil
probe	asks probing questions of pupil
	asks probing questions of other pupils

Effective responding includes giving reinforcement and feedback to your pupils. It is also associated with conveying enthusiasm and generating interest. Here there is a risk for the beginner. He or she might, unwillingly, react positively to all answers regardless of their merits. Used in this way, reinforcement and feedback can become meaningless and the structure and sequence of the lesson may be lost. The risk for experienced teachers is to respond in a mechanical way. Automatic smiling and set phrases may convey lack of interest in the lesson or pupils.

more fillings, because things you eat can affect your body.'

Sequencing questions

Sequencing questions is a subtle art. A set of individual questions may each be sound, but together produce cacophony. As indicated earlier, the lynch-pins of a sequence are often the responding moves of the teacher. The patterns that may emerge are shown in Figure 3.4. In the Leverhulme Project, we found that, out of more than 1000 questions

Figure 3.4 Sequences of questions (based on Brown and Edmondson 1984)

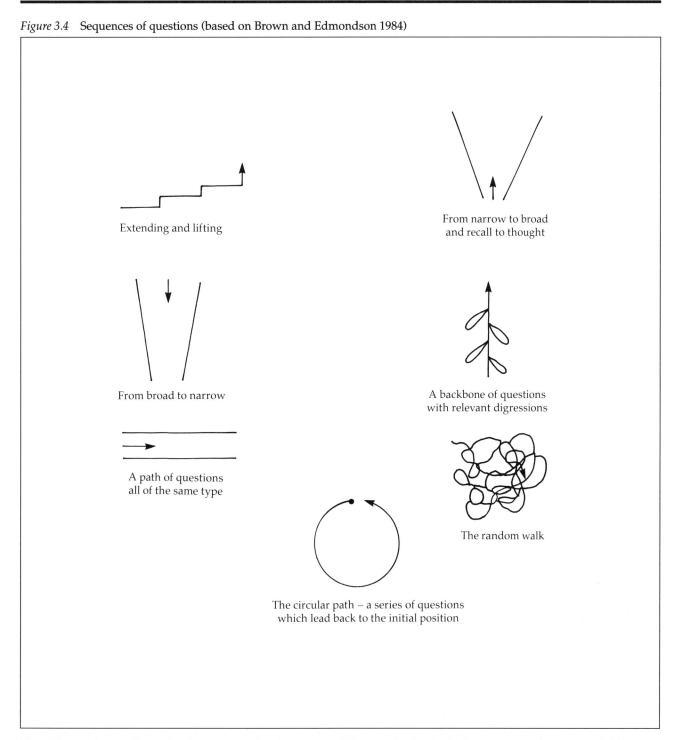

Extending and lifting

From narrow to broad
and recall to thought

From broad to narrow

A backbone of questions
with relevant digressions

A path of questions
all of the same type

The random walk

The circular path – a series of questions
which lead back to the initial position

Note: The random walk may be due to poor planning, personal disorganization in the lesson or very distracting children.

analysed, 53 per cent stood alone and 47 per cent were part of a sequence of two or more questions. Only 10 per cent of questions asked were in a sequence of more than four questions.

The notion of extending and lifting provided by Taba (1971) is particularly relevant here. Extending involves asking a series of questions at the same level before lifting the level of questions to the next higher level. Taba suggested that if pupils were to reach more complex levels of thought, they need ample opportunity to work at the lower levels by being asked for, or generating their own examples and solutions.

Transcripts of lessons from the Leverhulme

Project in which questions were thought to be used effectively suggest that teachers have in mind key questions around which are clustered a large number of briefer, more direct and specific questions. The lessons develop a pattern which may not always take a straight line, but which is certainly not random.

Keeping a lesson on course is a particular difficulty for newly qualified teachers. The temptation is to railroad the pupils in a way that is not appropriate, or to allow too much wandering away from the point of the lesson. A useful image here is tacking, as in sailing. You adjust your questioning so that you move through a lesson yet stay on course. The image also reminds us that to stay on course you need to know what the course is, hence the importance of planning sequences based on key questions and on preparing interesting material relevant to the questions being asked (see Unit 6).

ACTIVITY 8

1 Devise a sequence of four or five questions that could raise the level of thinking in a class. An example of a three-step sequence is:

Can you give me an example of something living?
What do plants need to help them grow?
How could we test out your idea that plants need water to grow?

2 Think about a sequence of questions that you have used recently. Which pattern in Figure 3.4 was it closest to? Using Figure 3.4, try planning one of the sequences (not the random walk) and using it in a lesson. Consider how well you kept to the sequence.

ACTIVITY 9

1 Look at these two statements and decide what different effects they would produce in an actual classroom:

a) 'Jill. What happens when these substances are heated together?'
b) 'Now what happens when these substances are heated together? Jill?'

2 Read the following transcripts and identify examples of prompts, probes and other features of the tactics of questioning.

Transcript 3.3

T: What do you remember about the legend of Robin Hood? Do you know anything about him?
P: He was in the woods.
T: That's right [pause] and what did he do?
P: Erm his bow and arrow.
T: Yes.
P: Trees and people.
T: What was he trying to do?
P: Trying to kill animals.
T: Was he? Wasn't he very nice then, Robin Hood?
P: No, not all the time, we watched a film about it. [Pause]
T: Who was his real enemy [pause] the Sheriff of ...?
P: The Sheriff of Not – Nott-ing-ham.
T: Do you remember who were his friends? Robin Hood had some really good friends, who was that big fat man Friar ...?
P: Friar erm erm.
P: Friar ... Tuck.
T: Yes!
T: You remember, and Little John who was his tall friend.

Transcript 3.4

(This is an upper primary class discussing *A Christmas Carol*)

T: What sort of a man was Scrooge? – Scott?
P: A stinge.
T: A stinge.
P: He didn't want to give his money away.
T: All right, he doesn't want to give any money away or anything – why?
P: Too grumpy.
T: He's a grumpy man, Mark, so he doesn't want anyone to feel happy, he doesn't want to give them anything, good!
P: Selfish.
T: Carl thinks he's selfish and indeed the centre of his life is himself.
P: He is unhappy because when he was younger his girlfriend left him and he didn't want anyone too.
T: That's absolutely true, something sad happened to him and they never really got together and never married and he became miserable, he became selfish, he lived for himself – yes April?

P: He's all stingy and tight and grumpy.
T: Stingy, tight and grumpy.
P: He doesn't care about anyone else.
T: Right, he doesn't care about anyone else – last one, John?
P: He like um er never got enough money.
T: Right – never got enough money for what?
P: To um, he's the sort of person who could never give money away to any charity.
T: Does that mean he does not give money away to charity because he's so poor himself, John?
P: No, he's so rich and so mean.
T: That's right, he's rich and he is mean. We do know that he is a successful businessman and actually he has got quite a lot of money but he keeps that money for himself.

3 Audio-record part of one of your lessons in which you are asking questions. Take four or five minutes of that audio-recording which contains questions and produce a transcript of them. Analyse the tactics of questioning that you used. Pay particular attention to your pausing, pacing, prompting and probing.
4 Here is the beginning of a scene in a classroom:

✳ **Transcript 3.5**

T: So that's heaven then is it? Does everybody go to heaven?
P: Yes.
T: Are you sure?
P: Yes.
T: Do grown ups go to heaven?
P: Yes.
T: Do children go to heaven?
P: Yes.
P: Miss! Miss!
T: Yes, Stacey?
P: My cat's died, Miss, and my cat died and my Mum said that my cat's gone to heaven, Miss, and it died and we put it and we buried it under a tree.

If you were the teacher what would you do next?

WHAT KINDS OF LESSONS DO YOU TEACH?

The whole of teaching and learning is shot through with the art of questioning.

(Hamilton 1928)

Before reading this unit you might like to tackle the following activity.

ACTIVITY 10

Spend a few minutes jotting down the various kinds of lessons that you have taught during the past few weeks. Compare your categories of lessons with those of a few colleagues. (The term 'lesson' is used here to include any structure for organizing learning, such as project work as well as conventional lessons.) What kind of lessons do you prefer? Why? What did you think of first when tackling this activity?

Some teachers report that in attempting this activity they first thought of lessons in terms of content rather than in terms of structure. Indeed it is difficult (but revealing) to attempt to classify lessons in terms of structures. It is salutary to discover that you are using the same basic structure for all your lessons – and only changing the content.

In this unit we describe four basic types of lessons which can be used in primary schools. These types are labelled 'exposition', 'discussion', 'skill' and 'investigative'. Within each type there are variations and sometimes what begins as one type of lesson may deliberately or unintentionally merge into another type. Usually unintentional drift is from exposition to random discussion with younger children, and from investigation to exposition with older children. Within each type teachers create their own structures, and the four types we discuss are not exclusive; there are many different types of lesson, including mixtures of type.

EXPOSITION LESSONS

In exposition lessons the teacher explains, asks questions and pupils answer. The lesson is often followed by individual learning tasks, although it can be followed by small group learning or investigations. The lesson may be a sequence of brief explanations and questions, or a chunk of exposition followed by lengthy questions and answers. The exposition may be based upon all forms of content, from science to legend. The pupils may be involved in various forms of learning: recitation, reasoning, imagining, speculating, evaluating.

Such lessons are known as recitation lessons in the United States (see Dillon 1988). They are as old as Socrates. They were used widely in the nineteenth century, in the early twentieth century and they are still in use today. There is no inherent weakness in such lessons, the weakness lies in using *only* these kinds of lessons. This point was addressed in the Cockcroft Report on mathematics:

Exposition by the teacher has always been a fundamental ingredient of work in the class room and we believe that this continues to be the case. We wish though to stress one aspect of it which seems often to be insufficiently appreciated. Questions and answers should constitute a dialogue. There is a need to take account of and to respond to the answers the pupils give to questions asked by the teacher as the exposition develops. Even if an answer is what one is hoping to receive it should not be ignored; exploration of a pupil's incorrect or unexpected response can lead to worthwhile discussion and increased awareness for both teacher and pupil of specific misunderstandings or misinterpretations.

(Cockroft 1982)

Despite the reservations about exposition lessons they do form a valuable function if handled

It follows that to make questions effective in exposition one needs to know one's topic and to estimate what the children may know or not know about it. The common error observed in the Leverhulme Project was that some teachers asked only questions to which virtually every child knew the answer. For example:

'Do you know what this is?'
'Miss, Miss, Miss – a butterfly'
'What are these?'
'Miss, Miss – its wings'

What do and don't pupils know?

sensibly. The broad purposes of questioning in exposition lessons are:

1 To encourage pupils to talk so they reveal what they already know and don't know.
2 To ensure that they have grasped the key points which link to earlier learning and which will link to subsequent learning.
3 To develop their understanding of what is being learnt.

Another common error in exposition is to ask only questions that come to mind. This takes a lesson to points not intended, so the teacher has to make an abrupt transition in questioning, which may puzzle the pupils who are trying to grasp the sense of what is being said. Or the teacher may launch into an unintended and perhaps confusing explanation, in order to salvage the lesson.

Figure 4.1 provides some suggestions for

Figure 4.1   Questioning in the exposition

- Convert your exposition into a series of key questions.
- Before asking the question, prepare the questions to ask.
- Ask the questions nice and slowly, stop and think whether the question is right for the occasion. Ask and stop.
- Listen to the answers, listen for the forthcoming answers, listen for all the answers, listen to right and wrong answers, sustain the listening.

---

improving the effectiveness of questions in exposition lessons. The suggestions are also relevant to other lessons. They are based upon suggestions in Dillon (1988).

'Stop and think' reminds us not to ask the question that pops into our heads but to consider it briefly to ensure that it is worth while. The question then has more chance of helping pupils to learn rather than encouraging them to open their mouths. 'Ask and stop' helps us to avoid asking too many questions and gives time for pupils to think before they answer.

Listening to the answers requires discipline. The answers that children give may not necessarily reveal what they know so much as what they think you want them to say. Their understanding may be imperfect but their answer is correct (Doyle 1983). Alternatively, they may have answered a different question from the one that you thought you had asked.

'Have you ever taken any drugs?' is a question that for some eleven-year-olds may have a different meaning to the one intended by the teacher in a science or health education lesson.

DISCUSSION LESSONS

Discussion lessons may be characterized as conversations that go back and forth, over and round a topic. There is not a rigid structure so much as a flexible framework to the lesson. Expositions that become unintentional discussions usually lack even that framework. Discussions tend to have fewer questions, more contributions from pupils and relatively more pupil/pupil exchanges – but still few in absolute terms. Discussion with small groups of pupils may be regarded as an important sub-set of discussion lessons, and these are discussed in the companion book in this series by Dunne and Bennett (1990). In both forms of discussion lessons there is a problem of identifying the key questions to be discussed and the identification of appropriate methods of organizing the discussion. Broadly speaking, you should think

about the key questions which you want to focus upon in the topic and then think of the questions that may be perplexing, intriguing or puzzling to pupils. The method of question adopted should be predominantly the use of encouraging, broad questions. This may begin with recall questions to extend and activate knowledge and then thought questions to lift the discussion. Some further suggestions on preparing discussion questions are given in Unit 6.

As well as using broad questions you can also use alternative questions. Some possibilities are given in Figure 4.2.

Using statements rather than questions is based on the notion that providing views and information can evoke more open responses. Even in everyday conversation it is difficult to ignore a statement (Hey, I'm talking to you!). However, making statements in classrooms requires you to think about the questions that spring to mind and then convert them into statements.

A common problem, during discussion with children, is getting lost. Put less bluntly, it is knowing how far to let the discussion move off its principal theme. The answer to this problem lies in the key question for the topic. If you cannot see the connection, then either move the discussion back on course, or ask a pupil how what he is saying is related to the question and the discussion.

SKILL LEARNING

Young teachers with little experience of teaching may take for granted a wide variety of skills that are learnt by children in the primary school. Tying shoe laces, combing hair, fastening buttons, washing hands and face, brushing teeth are but the simpler ones. More complex are swimming, trampolining, gymnastics, cycling, music, drawing, painting, writing and basic reading. Indeed skills, even if defined only as 'goal-directed sensori-motor activities', are the prerequisites in learning new methods and theories. For example, keyboard skills are required in computing; manipulative skills are the basis of setting up scientific apparatus and

'No, Darren, the key question is not "Do they actually pay you for teaching us this rubbish?" '

Figure 4.2   Alternatives to questions

1 Use a statement related to what the pupil has just said, and wait.
2 Review yours or other people's experiences with regard to the discussion.
3 Review yours or other people's feelings regarding the topic under discussion and ask a Why? question.
4 Indicate your acceptance of what a pupil has said and look to another pupil for a response.
5 Say nothing but look interested and thoughtful, so someone else is encouraged to talk.
6 Ask the pupils to ask questions of you and each other.
7 Encourage, paraphrase and summarize.

survey instruments. The teacher, as well as the pupils, often has to learn new sensori-motor skills such as using a video camera, setting up an overhead projector and audio-recording a class discussion. When we enlarge the scope of skill to include cognitive skills such as reading, writing, problem-solving and social skills, then skills become not just the basis but the centrepiece of much of our work.

All skills have components requiring us both to perceive and move in varying proportions. Copying from the blackboard is high on both perceiving and moving. Reading is higher on perceptual components. Skills usually are goal-directed: they contain built-in feedback, which enables us to adjust our actions to the tasks in hand, and they are patterned sequences of actions in response to cues rather than isolated instances of behaviour. Interested readers are referred to Patrick and Stammers (1975) for further details and to Harrow (1972) for a taxonomy of skills. In this section we focus upon the essentials of teaching someone else a skill and the use of questions and statements in such a task. Skill teaching may involve a whole class, a group of pupils or just one child. The basic principles, however, remain the same in these different circumstances. First, we have to analyse the task; second, to demonstrate; third, to provide the practice with guidance; fourth, to monitor and provide feedback. Think of acquiring a relatively simple skill, like threading a needle. We analyse the task (the thread must go through the eye of the needle), someone might demonstrate for us (including handy tips like licking the end of the thread), we practise, under supervision, and then someone tells us how well we are doing.

TASK ANALYSIS

This is the key to successful preparation for teaching skills. One has to analyse what is involved in this skill and then design a sequence of tasks which are meaningful to the pupils. There are four types of task which are common.

1 The pupil is required to do something he/she already knows but in a different learning context. (Switching on a computer and opening a programme.)
2 The pupil has to learn an entirely new pattern of responses en bloc. (Catching or hitting a ball. Copying a single letter.)
3 The pupil has to learn a new pattern of responses in a series of sub-tasks which are then joined together. (Hop, step and jump. Handwriting.)
4 The pupil has to combine the learning of new and old responses in response to patterns of cues. (Copying a drawing. Following a recipe.)

a ACTIVITY 11

Think of some examples of practical tasks that children tackle in the primary school. Classify them, using steps 1–4. Note that what is new to a five-year-old may be commonplace to a seven-year-old.

DEMONSTRATION

Demonstrating consists of cueing appropriate actions by providing a model, statements and questions. The task is not easy. Writing on the blackboard to demonstrate writing on paper is often not an effective model, because the movements required for writing on paper by a pupil are very different from those required for writing on a blackboard. The first step is to demonstrate the skill in its entirety and then, if possible, to break it down, slow it down and identify to the pupils what the salient cues are. Here you can use various observation questions such as 'Why do I hold the paper down with my hand? Why do I draw the pencil towards me and not away from me? Why do I write these letters big?'

GUIDANCE

The pupil now tries to imitate the teacher or other models while being provided with guidance. This may be in the form of positive statements such as 'Press lightly' rather than negative guidance such as 'Don't press too hard.' Much of guidance is in fact concerned with getting pupils to watch for the cues: 'Keep your eye on the ball' is a useful shorthand statement for much of the advice to give to pupils on learning skills. You can use questions that develop understanding of the skills, such as 'Why should you only press on lightly? Why should you hold your pencil firmly but not too firmly?'

An alternative approach to direct guidance is to ask the pupil to give you the instructions and you to carry them out with guidance from him or her. This approach can help pupils to identify and reduce many errors and it can also be fun.

FEEDBACK AND QUESTIONS

It is commonplace knowledge that precise relevant knowledge of results and positive feedback improve learning; it is, unfortunately, not always common practice. One reason for this is that, to be able to provide precise relevant knowledge of results, you must have conducted an analysis of the task so that you can point to the salient cues. As well as providing knowledge of results and feedback you can also use questions to help a pupil to analyse his or her own performance. For example:

What should you do with your other hand when you are writing?
Which way did you draw that Z?

Was it the right way? Now try going backwards across and back again.

What is different about these two letters? Could you draw over them? Now tell me what is different.

INVESTIGATIVE LEARNING

Investigative learning involves experimentation or finding out by pupils. There are many forms of investigative learning and they vary in time spent on task, on the degree of openness of the task. Some examples are simple experiments or studies in primary science or history. More complex examples are projects by individuals and groups. Within the framework of investigative learning we can

Figure 4.3 Levels of experiment

	Level	Aim	Materials	Method	Answer
Demonstration	0	Given	Given	Given	Given
Exercise (Recipe)	1	Given	Given	Given	Given
Structured Enquiry	2	Given	Given	Part or Whole	Open or Part Given
Open Enquiry	3	Given	Open	Open	Open
Project	4	Open	Open	Open	Open

distinguish levels of experiments (see Figure 4.3).

Small-scale but not large-scale projects in primary schools are likely to be at level 2. Many teachers who are not confident about their science or maths teaching often opt for demonstration rather than enquiry. Some teachers in the Leverhulme Study chose deliberately to use open-ended approaches so that they could learn with their pupils and from their pupils, especially when they are on unfamiliar ground in fields such as science and technology.

Investigative learning requires the use of a wide variety of thought questions. Among these are speculative questions, evaluative questions and reasoning questions. These questions need to be planned and incorporated into the investigation. So again preparation is important (see Unit 6).

All of this raises important questions about the role of the teacher in different circumstances. During investigative lessons or learning sequences the role of teacher moves closer to that of manager, adviser, guide, supporter and improver. These tasks are given in more detail in Figure 4.4. The roles indicated in Figure 4.4 may overlap, but they do provide a series of pointers for the way in which we might tackle investigative lessons. In addition to asking questions, however, teachers also have to carry out a number of activities which help pupils to learn on the spot. These are listed in Figure 4.5.

 **ACTIVITY 12**

1 In the following transcript, Claire, a nine-year-old pupil, answers the question fully. If no answer had been forthcoming, what sequence of questions would you have asked to obtain the information that Claire provided?

✳ Transcript 4.1

T: 'Right, we are going to ask Mrs Cox about this Neighbourhood Watch Scheme. Now what was one of the first questions that we were going to ask her – Claire? What is it?'

P: Well it's a scheme really that all the people living in your road look after each other's houses really to make sure that nobody is going around stealing anything or breaking into houses which we hope won't happen but also just keeping an eye open, watching anything suspicious that happens in your road that you might think will help the Police solve a crime really. So any cars that you might see parked that aren't usually there, or people around, take a note of their number and the Police come round every now and then and check with you to see if anything has happened in your street or road, and then they make a note of it and sometimes they can solve crimes. Really just to look after your houses and keep everything safe and do it for each other, and if somebody goes away on holiday you can say Oh! we know Mrs Smith is away so we will keep an eye on her house, that's what it's about, so you know what the Neighbourhood Watch Scheme is now.

2 Read the two transcripts that follow and compare the teacher's use of questions. Who seemed to be the better questioner in this context and why?

Figure 4.4   Roles of the teacher in investigative lessons

Director	Determining topic and method, providing ideas.
Facilitator	Providing access to resources and arranging programme of work.
Adviser	Helping to resolve problems and suggesting alternatives.
Teacher	Providing instruction when it is necessary.
Guide	Suggesting timetable for carrying out the investigation, writing up, giving feedback on progress and so on.
Critic	Commenting constructively upon the way the pupils are carrying out the investigation or interpreting the data.
Freedom giver	Giving pupils the opportunity to take decisions for themselves.
Supporter	Giving encouragement, showing interest, discussing pupils' ideas.
Manager	Checking progress regularly, monitoring what is going on, giving systematic feedback and helping the pupils to plan their work.
Examiner	Examining and appraising pupils' work and showing them at the end of the investigation how it could be improved even further.

Figure 4.5   Some tasks for the teacher in investigative lessons

- Anticipate and recognize the major difficulties that pupils experience.
- Ask questions that clarify understanding.
- Ask questions that clarify actions.
- Ask questions that guide the pupils to do the right things.
- Answer questions in a simple non-condescending way.
- Offer support and encouragement.
- Know when to help and when not to help.

✤ Transcript 4.2

T: Let's just recap a little bit on what we have been doing. We started off with flight didn't we, making what? Gliders first of all and we were using the air around us to make these things fly weren't we? Can anyone remember what we learned about that? Right, if it had a pointed nose that was aerodynamic, that was the suggestion. What does aerodynamic mean then? It's a very good word and a very important concept, what does it mean? The wind can pass through? Is that right? Cut through? Getting closer.

P: Cut over it.

T: Cut over it – yes! Do you actually mean that – the wind will cut through it or do you mean the dart itself will cut through the air? Right. So we found out that the shape was very important, wasn't it? Later on we will be finding out a little bit more about wind and how different shapes make a difference and we'll move on from there. From the paper darts we moved on to parachutes. What did you find out about air and parachutes – Nigel?

P: The air held up the parachute?

T: Right! What was pulling the parachute down?

P: Gravity.

T: Yes – weight, gravity was pulling it down. The weight, do you remember the parachute – what shape was it as it was falling? Do you remember somebody drew one pointed and we said that was wrong, didn't we? It was oval-shaped.

P: Like a semi-circle.

T: A semi-circle, good. Why was it like that then, Sarah?

P: . . . . . . [inaudible]

T: Right! That's right. The air that was going into the parachute made the parachute expand at the top. Can you actually remember why we put a hole in the top of a parachute? Why did we put a hole in the top – Peter? Speak up so we can hear – why did we put a hole in the top?

P: To balance.

T: So it was balanced, good boy, well done! That's right, without it he couldn't keep his balance and he would move around. The hole in the top controls the air going out, doesn't it? Now we are moving on today, we are going to look at how we have used air, things that have moved through air and how we can use air, but today I want to introduce you to something else, the fact that air itself can move and we can use that air. What do we call first of all, what do we call moving air outside? We've had a lot of it during the last few weeks, come on! It's obvious, Nicky.

P: Wind.

T: Wind. Right. Good. Moving air is called wind.

Giving pupils the opportunity to take decisions for themselves

Can wind affect our movements, can it affect movement? Pardon?

✳ Transcript 4.3

T: Now. The first thing, we did this a little while ago, what we are going to think about this afternoon is why it is that birds can fly and we can't. Now what was one reason that we looked at after we looked at the TV programme. We had a go at doing something, what did we do, can anyone remember?

P: We made some flaps of our own and tried to get 3000 in five minutes.

T: 3000 flaps in a minute, wasn't it? Who was it that could do 3000 flaps in one minute? Marina?

P: A bird.

T: Can you remember which bird?

P: A humming bird.

T: Right! It's a humming bird that could actually get 3000 flaps in a minute. How close could we get to that?

P: I did 250.

P: 300.

T: 300. Well I think some of our memories may be a little bit rusty, so we'll have another go. So stand up in a space so you're not too close to anyone and don't start until I tell you or you'll be worn out. I'll say: on your marks, get set, go. Now stop, right sit down in your places again. Right. The first question I want to ask John is, how many birds have you seen that keep their wings still at the beginning and just flap the ends of them like you were doing?

P: He's always doing that!

T: Right. Sssh. How many did you manage, Marina?

P: 105.

T: Not bad. What about you, Alice?

P: 124.

T: Pretty good! Helena?

P: [no reply]
T: David?
P: 206.
T: Pretty good! Adam?
P: 1000.
T: 1000! Are you sure? My goodness! You really must be aching, what about you?
P: 140.
T: That's pretty good, Lee.
P: 300.
P: He was counting in tens!
T: John with your sort of half wings how many did you do?
P: 112.
T: Stuart, what about you?
P: 1000.
T: Are you sure? I think some of your counting methods have gone a bit astray there! Right. Did any of us manage 3000?
P: No.
P: Nearly.
T: Not quite. Why can't we manage 3000?
P: Our muscles aren't big enough.
T: How big are your muscles, David? Where are your muscles?
P: Here.
P: Everywhere.
T: What are muscles for?
P: To make sure you can move.
T: How do they work?
P: If you didn't have any muscles you would just be flab and if you have got muscles then you can jump around and all that.
T: Oh, very good! Thank you very much, John. We've got a picture here, let's see the picture for a minute and let's see if we can actually find a muscle and see what it's doing. Find this muscle here and rest your hand on top of it'. [puts hand on biceps]
P: Mine can go really high.
T: How do you make it go really high then John?
P: You've just got to flex it up and turn it round.
T: That's right. Bring your arm up, can you feel it? Right. Let's give everyone a chance because you're all screaming at once, I can't hear what Alice and Marina are saying. Can you find yours, Alice?'
P: Yes!

3 Audio record a brief exposition lesson. Transcribe a few minutes of it where questions and answers were in use, and in particular if a question-and-answer session went off course. Consider what alternative questions or responses you could have made during this sequence of your transcript to try to bring the lesson back on course or to improve the pattern of questions. This activity is best done by a group of teachers. They might read each other's transcripts and offer alternative suggestions and comments on strategies.

4 Read the following extract from a discussion lesson and comment on the teacher's ways of encouraging the pupils to talk. The lesson was about the relationships between ethnic groups. One pupil observed that black policemen had a hard time. The following discussion ensued. (The lesson was for 10–11 year-olds.)

❋ **Transcript 4.4**

T: That's a good point actually. It must be difficult.
P: The thing is if the black Police Officers try it with the white ones so that they actually think that they have to put up this sort of er, er, image and say well erm I'm not really black.
T: Like this?
P: Yes.
T: Yes?
P: Yes, they should just be themselves really.
T: But it's so easy to say isn't it? You would have to be a very strong person to do that wouldn't you?
P: Yes, people won't talk to them and it's hard to work with people that won't talk to you and things like that.
T: Yes.
P: Because they've got to be two different people. They've got to be sort of someone at work and someone at home who's not a Policeman.
T: Yes.
P: So erm, it must be really difficult.
P: Yeah, they've got to leave their work at work and just be themselves at home.
T: Yes.

5 Here is an extract from a transcript in an art lesson. The children are learning to use palettes. Identify the demonstration, instructions and questions and the guidance questions. How would you have tackled this lesson? Compare your views with those of a few colleagues.

❋ **Transcript 4.5**

T: Do Emma's apron up for her please. Then, Emma, will you do Paul's apron up for him, good. You're going to read to yourself. Go and sit down and enjoy yourself. Can you do it? Good boy, now she's going to do yours. This is a new way of painting and you need one of these things called a palette, so you can hold on to your palettes. Right. We haven't got any colours yet on the palette, have we?

P: No.

T: That's yours over there, Paul, and we've got a clean brush. Now, what you need to do with your mixing paints, you need to have a wet brush so you put your paintbrush in the water, is it nice and wet? Wipe it on the side so it doesn't drip. Now choose a colour, see what different colour greens you can make. So if you start by getting some green on your brush and putting it on your palette in a space. Is that green, Wayne? You can have mine, there you are, that's it, and when you've got a nice lot of green on there, right, give the brush a wash in the water so it's nice and clean. Don't forget to wipe it on the side so it doesn't drip. Is it clean? You've got no green left on it. Choose another colour to add to your green, any colour you like, yellow or blue or white. To put with the green, yes, on your palette, that's it! You're having blue are you? That's lovely! Take as much as you want and then when you want some water in it, so this time when you put your brush in the water let some water come out with it so it will drip like this into your palette, and then you can mix it up and see what you make. Is it easier to put your palette down on the ground? You see I am holding mine up here because it's easier for me to show you. Good, right. Let's put all our palettes together and have a quick look shall we? Look at all the different greens we've made. Paul, can you bring yours here a minute, we're having a look to see what colours we have made. Yours is a different colour from mine, isn't it? Yours is darker, yours is a lovely dark green. Would you like to paint with that colour now on your paper? Would you like to paint me something on your paper with that colour you've made? If you want to change the colour then you can add some water can't you after you have washed your brush. Let's see how many lovely colours you can make. That's good! What happens to your colour when you add more yellow to it?

P: It goes dark green.

T: Pardon! How many colours have you got there?

6 Write a script of about two pages based on an exposition, discussion, skill or investigative lesson. Be adventurous and funny if you wish. Swop with a colleague and analyse the questions and responses used in each other's lessons.

7 Design and teach a brief investigative lesson. Identify the level of investigation that you are aiming at. Design some discussion questions based on the investigation. At the end of the lesson, provide a brief summary (mini-exposition). If possible, work on this activity with a colleague so that you can observe and discuss the purposes, design questions and analyse the questions actually asked in the lessons. An added useful activity is to draw up a checklist of tactics that you would like your colleague to observe. For example, your use of pupil's ideas in developing the exposition summary.

8 Read this extract from a science lesson. What were the purposes of the questions? How could the exposition be improved?

✳ Transcript 4.6

T: What I'd like to do this afternoon is continue what we were doing yesterday. What did we do yesterday with these blocks?

P: We got these weights and this little rope thing, tied it on the rope and then we put some weights on it to see how many weights it would drag down and we took forty for that one.

T: What's it called? Does anybody know what it's called that drags on the top of it?

P: Friction.

T: Friction! Brilliant! So what is friction? Sarah, do you know?

P: No.

T: Edward?

P: When it gets really hot.

T: It doesn't always get hot.

P: Sometimes it's static.

T: Lindsay?

P: Friction is when you rub your hands together like that and they get really hot.

T: What I'm going to ask you when we have finished the experiment today is how we have used friction in these experiments, so think about that. I'm going to say not just what is friction but what is it with reference to this experiment. All right? Now what I want you to do using these blocks is, I want you to find out the most efficient way of actually getting them moving. When I say efficient what do I mean? I mean the easiest way to get them to move so

Independent investigation

what could you do to test that? Nick – how are we going to find the easiest way of getting it to move?

P: [Answer inaudible]

T: What I want you to do is, do you remember how we discussed it? That it would be easier rather than to drag it along the table to roll it on things, on straws or pencils. We didn't try rolling it on cotton reels or loo rolls or anything like that. I want you to find the easiest way of getting it to move. Now, how are we going to decide whether it's the easiest way or not?

P: We could see which takes the most weights.

T: The most weights?

P: Yes.

T: Deborah, what was that?

P: The less weights.

T: Yes! The less weights. Obviously if it only takes 10 grammes to get it moving then it's easier than if it takes 40 grammes isn't it? So let's get going. You've got the same again as yesterday, there are all different things on the bottom of the friction box. Swop them round so you get at least two different things.

---

9 Re-write some of the questions and explanations in the transcript above so that they would be more clear to the pupils. Compare your suggested improvements with those of a few colleagues.

HOW DO YOUR CHILDREN LEARN?

Nothing is in the mind that is not already in the senses.

(Aristotle)

This Unit is about how your children learn and how you can use questions to help them to learn. It is not about theories of learning or child development. Readers interested in these matters are referred to Hergenhahn (1988). Here, we focus upon what you can do to help your children to learn. We also believe that it is vital for children to be brought in on the act of reflection. If teachers reflect on questioning and pupils' answers, why shouldn't children? Some of the Activities in this Unit invite and provide structure for teachers to think about questions and answers with their classes. We begin by inviting you to consider these questions.

ⓐ ACTIVITY 13

Jot down your thoughts on the following:
1 How do the children in your class learn?
2 What prevents them from learning?
3 How do they learn best?
Compare your thoughts with those of a few colleagues.

You may have discovered, in describing the ways that your children learn, that you also articulated your personal theory of learning and teaching. Look carefully at your classroom teaching to see how well it matches your claims ...

Sometimes the personal theory of learning arises out of our practice rather than our reading. More precisely, personal theories of learning are in part manifest and in part determined by the way we teach. They can be circular and self-fulfilling, for the way we teach shapes the way the pupils respond and learn, which, in its turn, confirms our views of how pupils learn. For example, if we ask mostly questions that require simple factual recall then most pupils will produce only factual answers. So we might conclude that children are only capable of providing factual answers. This may lead on to the view that children do not think and to the judgement that children are lazy intellectually.

As indicated earlier we don't want to recite to you various theories of learning but we do want you to explore your own theory of learning, so we offer you six guidelines to consider, modify and extend.

1 Your approaches to teaching

In Unit 4 we discussed briefly the use of questions in some common lessons – exposition, discussion, skill learning and investigative learning. The question that you might ask yourself is 'What is the most appropriate type of lesson and style of questioning for the task in hand and this particular group of children?' Given also the importance of interest and involvement, then a variety of approaches is most appropriate. As Bennett (1976) indicated, the better teachers often considered the children's interests as well as the task. Similar remarks apply to the use of questions. A wide variety of types and levels of questions is important for interesting children and helping them develop.

2 Active learning

Most children (and adults) learn best when actively involved. So it is useful to look at the range of activities that pupils do in your classroom. Just as variety is the key to good teaching and questioning, so it is also the essence of active learning.

3 Purposive learning

Activity per se is not enough. Children (and adults) learn best when they know what is expected of them. In some of the lessons that we observed in the Leverhulme Project, many of the children were active but unsure of what they were supposed to be doing. The expressed aims of many of these poorer lessons were laudable but often vague:

> 'To widen the horizons of experience'.
> 'A study of the history and social development of the wheel'.

In contrast, in the successful lessons teachers had realistic, concrete objectives about what the children would be learning:

> 'Get children to think about what it must be like to be ...'
> 'To familiarize them with the methods ...'
> 'To get them to do ...'
> 'To develop their ability to observe how people look ...'

4 Safe learning

Children (and adults) learn best when they feel safe enough to take risks in their learning. Hence the importance of class management, of well-defined procedures and routines (see the volume in this series, *Class Management*, Wragg 1993). Indeed, the absence of a safe secure structure is probably the major obstacle to children learning in the classroom. Managerial questions, including reminders of the procedures, are relevant here.

5 Reflective learning

Reflective learning may at first sight seem only possible for mature learners. Yet it is at least arguable that reflective learning should begin in the primary school, so that children learn to analyse, evaluate and explore their actions and thoughts. Much of reflective learning is based upon thought questions, and hence it is important for us to consider the thought questions we are going to ask our children if we wish to develop their reflective learning. Reflective learning includes considering two sorts of questions, How am I doing? How did I

do it? The first is related to self-assessment and the second to the processes of learning. The second is also related to an analysis of what it is to learn.

6 Responsible learning

Children (and adults) learn best when they have a sense of responsibility and ownership for their own learning. So encouraging children to organize and monitor their own learning is a valuable long-term objective. But there is a risk of confusing goals and means; it does not follow that, because responsibility is a long-term objective, we should make children solely responsible for their learning from day one. Rather, it is important to teach them to be responsible learners through our methods of teaching, learning tasks, encouragement and feedback. It should be obvious by now that the use of questions is central to this endeavour.

ACTIVITY 14

1 Keep a log for two days of the kinds of teaching that you did. You may use our categories of exposition, discussion, skill and investigative learning, or your own categories plus additional categories of when the children are working on their own or in groups. For this purpose, divide your day into quarter-hour segments and record the major activity within each segment. Record from time to time a question you have asked. Analyse the proportion of time devoted to each activity. Compare your profile with that of a few colleagues. Keeping a log is time-consuming, not to be recommended as a regular practice, as it takes away valuable teaching time. Once in a while, however, it can be a worthwhile activity.

9.00
9.15
9.30
9.45
10.00
10.15
10.30
10.45
11.00
11.15
11.30
11.45
12.00
12.15

Responsible learning

12.30
12.45
1.00
1.15
1.30
1.45
2.00
2.15
2.30
2.45
3.00
3.15
3.30
3.45
4.00
4.15
4.30
4.45

2 Here is a list of pupil tasks set or encouraged by teachers. Tick any that you used during the two days that you logged (see question 1) and add them to the list. Again, compare the tasks with those set or encouraged by your colleagues. These activities are by no means comprehensive.

 ACTIVITY 15

1 This transcript was taken from a lesson in which the class were not attending and the teacher was distracted. Read the transcript to establish what the teacher was trying to do. How would you have tackled the task? If you had stopped the lesson, because of poor attentiveness, what sort of questions might you have asked the pupils?

✻ **Transcript 5.1   The Badger**

P: Miss, there's a certain way to stroke a badger.
T: Before we go any further you need your reading book so if you haven't got it in a moment, don't go yet, reading book you need, you need the two pieces of paper I have given you, a pen or pencil whichever you feel comfortable writing with, a ruler for your margins, you can share a ruler if somebody's got it on the table and you've forgotten one, put them on now, both sides and write your name on the top. What do you need, a pencil? Here we go, do it on both

Figure 5.1   Some pupil activities

> 1 Doing work sheets.
> 2 Working with programmed or computer-based material.
> 3 Copying notes from the board.
> 4 Writing work book exercises.
> 5 Doing sums and mathematics problems.
> 6 Summarizing the thought of a plan.
> 7 Group discussions.
> 8 Guided reading in response to a question.
> 9 Completing multiple-choice true/false tests.
> 10 Writing a brief report.
> 11 Preparing material for a class magazine.
> 12 Carrying out experiments.
> 13 Writing up experiments as a group.
> 14 Demonstrating to other pupils.
> 15 Writing stories.
> 16 Preparing questions on what is being studied.
> 17 Preparing display materials for use around the classroom.
> 18 Looking for facts in a book.
> 19 Analysing data collected in the field or in the classroom.
> 20 Preparing charts or models.
> 21 Illustrating or representing ideas pictorially.
> 22 Map making or completing.
> 23 Short practice drills.
> 24 Estimating answers in mathematics or science before calculating them.
> 25 Making graphs or pictures from data given.
> 26 Translating written problems into mathematics.
> 27 Forming written problems on the basis of mathematics.
> 28 Seeking applications of scientific principles to everyday life.
> 29 Measuring.
> 30 Reporting on events.
> 31 Organizing facts and principles gathered from discussion.
> 32 Developing a map of the home community.
> 33 Identifying the kinds of people who live in your community.

sides and then you'll be ready. It doesn't matter if you don't write both sides, you've got it if you need it. Piece of paper for you, close this book up a minute, right there you are close this up. Put your name on the top, no, OK that's the business side of getting ready. You've got your paper ready and your name is on the top. If you haven't put your name on the top it doesn't matter which side you put the name on the top now. They're in the way, Tim, put them down on the floor, down there, don't worry about it, all you need is your name. No don't worry about the date and put down anything that you were using to write with because then I want you to listen to me. Right! now I know you are all listening when you are looking at me. Right. Just a few people I'm waiting for. Right, Tim, Kevin are you ready? If you look at me then I know that you are ready. Good boy! Turn round a little bit. Now yesterday in the afternoon we did an awful lot of talking, I did a lot of talking and we looked at a video and we looked at our badger. Now today for our piece of writing you are going to be thinking about the badger. You're going to be thinking about the badger in lots and lots of ways. You can decide what kind of way you would like to write your piece of writing, it could be that you're going to write me a story, it could be that you're the kind of person who likes to write facts. Now your piece of writing is going to be your choice, but I'm going to put lots of ideas to you and you could put some ideas back to me in a minute. Hands down until I'm ready. But your piece of writing is going to be your choice, but I'm going to put lots of ideas to you and you could put some ideas back to me in a minute. Hands down until I'm ready. But your piece of writing today, remember what we spoke about yesterday, is going to be your best piece of writing because it's going to go in your file. All right? So you're going to do your neatest writing, not worrying too much about spelling but thinking about it and thinking Yes, I think I know that word. All right, but don't worry if you can't spell it, put the nearest spelling that you know. Wait a minute – think about doing the best piece of work that you've done for a long time. All right? Now let's think about what we could write about badgers. No! Remember from yesterday how I said don't call out. Put your hand up if you've got an idea. That would be a very good piece to do because you could do the badger's fears and the kind of environment he was in where he was running to or where he was hiding. Lots of description could come into that.

2 *Children's Questions* If we concentrate too much on teachers' philosophies and teachers' questions, we may ignore children's questions and beliefs. This exercise will enable you to compare the sorts of questions children ask with those that teachers ask. There is no reason why children should not think about questions, just as teachers must! Give a group of children a set of objects or photographs of people. Ask them to list (or to state, if they are too young to write it down) as many questions about the objects or photographs as they can think of. Write down the questions on the board and then help children to categorize the kinds of questions that they have asked. Before you do this activity make sure you have jotted down some of your own questions, such as you ask pupils in the class. You can then compare, both privately and in class, your questions and children's questions. What is the same? What is different? And why?

3 Answers to questions are also something that should be shared with pupils. The following activity may be used with older primary pupils. Its purpose it to get them to consider what counts as good answers.

i) Set a simple exercise on a topic requiring pupils to give their views. Example: Write a brief answer, not more than 5–10 lines on 'Why do children go to school?'

ii) Before the pupils hand in their answers, put up on the blackboard three or four answers of differing quality. Ask the pupils to read the answers and to try to decide which is best and why. Develop a discussion on this theme. You will probably have to use all the skills described earlier in this text. Summarize the main points of what constitutes good answers to the question 'Why do children go to school?' (or your chosen topic).

iii) Ask the children to amend their answers in the light of the discussion. This could be done as their next homework exercise. Answer another simple thought question based upon the topic.

iv) Mark their answers carefully, praise their good points and suggest ways of improving upon their answers. You may find the following checklist helpful to you and your pupils:

Checklist

a Is my answer clear? Am I using understandable English in the answers and not confusing the person who is listening to me, or reading my answer?

b Is my answer accurate? Have I given facts and figures that are not true?

c Is my answer appropriate? Have I answered the question that was asked?

Maths: how did they arrive at the answers?

d Is my answer specific? Will the teacher or the person reading my answer know who and what I am writing about?

e Does my answer contain support for my views? Have I given reasons, facts or examples to support my opinions or argument?

f Does my answer show an awareness of complexity? Have I looked at more than one side of the question?

If possible, discuss individually with pupils their answers and your reactions to them.

4 How do you encourage your pupils to take responsibility for their own learning?

5 The following activity may be used with a small group of pupils or an individual pupil. Find a pupil or a set of pupils who have produced some wrong answers in a mathematics class. Ask a series of non-threatening questions aimed at discovering how they arrived at their answers. (Asking them to say aloud what they did may be sufficient for a simple task.) On the basis of this diagnosis, talk through what they should have done, using a series of questions and answers in the pupils' own language. Provide them with practice examples, in which you talk them through what they have to do and then they talk you through what you have to do when you are doing the same sorts of problems. Repeat this activity again and then reflect upon how you might improve your approach to it.

ARE YOU 'PREPARED' TO ASK QUESTIONS?

If you don't know where you are going, it is difficult to select a suitable means of getting there.

(Mager 1962)

In this Unit we explore the preparation of questions and, because we cannot prepare questions without considering the context and purposes of the lesson in which the questions occur, we also consider lesson preparation.

PREPARING QUESTIONS

As a preliminary to preparing questions, it is useful to consider these two questions:

1 What can I ask them?
2 What should I ask them?

A useful approach to 'What can I ask them?' is to brainstorm the questions. Take a blank sheet of paper and write down on it as many questions as you can within ten minutes – do not worry about the appropriateness or quality of the questions at this stage. Once you have done this, you can begin to sift the questions and arrive at what questions you will ask the pupils. Inevitably this leads you to consider what your objectives are and what the children might already know.

USING KEY QUESTIONS

Many teachers use *key questions* to structure and summarize their lessons. For example, in a lesson for nine-year-olds on badgers the key questions were 'What do they look like, What do they eat and drink, Where do they live?' The questions: 'Who are badgers related to? What kinds of badgers are there?

How do they live?' can also be considered, particularly with slightly older children. Their answers, of course, are likely to be more sophisticated than those of younger children.

Some teachers in the Leverhulme Project did not seem to use key questions well. A few appeared to think that key questions were any questions asked, others that the only key question was what the pupils would do. However, other teachers provided key questions and detail. Under detail, they also included self-instructions such as:

> 'Remind the pupils what they already know.'
> 'Stress the importance of silence while writing.'
> 'Insist on paragraph structures.'
> 'Make sure Rosy is working.'

The first key question asked by teachers in the project was usually a 'What' question, although 'How', 'Why', 'Do you think', 'Which would you' were also used. It would be tempting to say that 'What' questions got poor answers and 'How' questions were thought-provoking. In fact, 'What' questions produced both poor (unanswerable, dull, pointless) statements and good (stimulating, enjoyable, multi-faceted) responses. 'How' questions were also either thought-provoking or pointless. It was the content of the question in relation to the children, not its form, that determined its success.

The same can be said of the succeeding key questions in a lesson. Below are a few pointers from our analysis of the transcripts, which may help you when you are considering your own use of key questions.

Timing

Here are some key questions we observed, with comments on their timing.

'What is friction?' was asked by the teacher in a science lesson too early. It was asked before the investigation and it should have been asked and discussed after the children had some experience of the experiments on friction.

'What is a neighbourhood watch scheme?' The children had already done some work on this before the question was asked, and they could tell the teacher some good stories about neighbourhood watch schemes.

'How do you think it felt?' The children had experienced the sense of drama and impending threat to the character in the story. The pupils' answers were imaginative and these answers seemed to stimulate other pupils to provide imaginative answers also.

Key questions need not be asked at the beginning of a segment of a lesson. Indeed, they may be used to summarize what the children have just learnt, so do be wary of asking your key questions too early. And don't be afraid of asking thought questions of younger children at the right time. One teacher asked six-year-olds these questions:

'Why do tomatoes have more jelly stuff round them than other fruits?' and *'Do bigger fruits always have bigger seeds?'*

Level We have mentioned earlier some points about *levels* of questioning and the proper language register and thought processes appropriate to different circumstances. Here are further questions we have witnessed, with comments on level.

'What do we call frozen water . . .?' This question was too easy for ten-year-olds. Some teachers asked only questions that everybody could answer. Repeating these questions, as some teachers did, does not work well.

'How could you design a home for these owls?' Too difficult for eight-year-olds. The children floundered and couldn't sort out what was required of them. The question needed breaking down into separate components. They did not have the necessary experience to reply properly.

'What is the difference between a wing and an arm?' This looked like a mind-boggling question to young pupils, but in fact it worked well because the children were able to identify several

differences and the teacher then was able to help the children to classify them.

The best key questions contained a sense of looking ahead, of helping the lesson to move on. The least effective seemed to be going nowhere or only back to what the children already knew.

Our suggestions for use of key questions are encapsulated in the mnemonic IDEA, given in Figure 6.1.

PREPARING LESSONS

Most textbooks on teaching advocate the setting of objectives, choice of methods of teaching, pupil tasks and assessment. What these texts do not tell you is that few teachers actually plan their lessons in this order, although the product may be expressed in this form. The thinking processes involved in lesson preparation are less tidy and often more creative than a direct application of teaching by behavioural objectives (see Clarke and Petersen 1986).

The preparation of lessons may be construed in the form of three questions:

1 What do I want my pupils to learn?
2 How do I want them to learn it?
3 How will I find out whether they have learnt it?

Using a mind map

Most teachers approach these questions through considering content and:

> experience
> activities
> methods

A **mind map** is a helpful way into these questions (see Figure 6.2). To do this you write down the topic of a lesson in the centre of a page and then write down a set of sub-topics or questions around the topic. This may lead to further division of the sub-topics or to another sub-topic. The next step is to redraw or tidy up the mind map, so that similar topics are clustered together. At this stage you can begin to identify the key questions that might structure the lesson. Note that these particular key questions are not necessarily the questions that you might ask the pupils. Some of them may be the questions that underlie the questions that you are going to ask.

A mind map provides the basis for thinking about any kind of topic or lesson. It may also be used during a lesson to move discussion on, to keep on

Figure 6.1   IDEA on questions

> **I**   Identify the key questions in relation to your objectives for the lesson.
>
> **D**   Decide on the level and order (timing) of the questions.
>
> **E**   Extend the questioning. Think of supplementary and subsidiary questions to ask.
>
> **A**   Analyse the answers that you are likely to receive and the responses that you might give.

'So, what have we learnt about electricity today, then?'

track and to summarize. Once the mind map is completed, the next step is the choice of pupil task and the method of teaching. This brings us to the question, 'How am I going to get them to learn it?' To answer this question, you may have to rummage through materials, ideas in your own head or invent new learning materials. Then comes the choice of method of teaching – although often you move between thinking about pupils' learning methods and the teaching methods. Last, but not least, you have to build into the tasks the opportunities to find out what the pupils have learnt. These include the use of oral questions, assessing project group and individual work.

The GAITO Approach

An alternative or supplementary approach to the use of a mind map is the GAITO approach:

Goals, Activities, Input, Timing, Order.

In this approach you consider what you want the pupils to learn their goals and the activities that you want them to undertake. You then consider what specific contributions you will make through exposition and questions. Estimate the time required for each segment – and allow for slippage. Consider then the order of the lesson. Incidentally, often the last thing you think of is the first thing

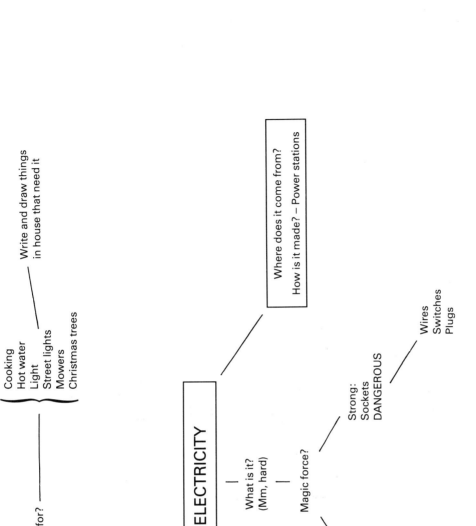

Write and draw things
in house that need it

Cooking
Hot water
Light
Street lights
Mowers
Christmas trees

What do we need it for?

Play

Story

Power cut

ELECTRICITY

What is it?
(Mm, hard)

Magic force?

Experiments?

Where does it come from?
How is it made? – Power stations

Strong:
Sockets
DANGEROUS

Wires
Switches
Plugs

Weak:
Batteries

Torches
Games
Toy cars
Personal stereos
Radios
Milk vans

The beginnings of a mind map

that you should do in a lesson. Consider also various pathways through the materials, for your pupils may not respond quite as you expect. You cannot predict accurately how a particular lesson will develop, but you can be prepared for most developments.

Finally, it is worth pointing out that most teachers find preparing topics or themes easier than

ACTIVITY 16

1 Prepare a lesson on a topic of your choice. Include at least four *key questions*. How do you think children will respond to them?
2 Audio-record the lesson. Before listening to the

Figure 6.3 A student's first attempt at a lesson planning record

<u>Time</u>: 15 minutes — Taken with pupils

<u>Topic</u>: Coleraine area. To learn the location of the main physical features of Coleraine, the growth of new housing, the social geography of the area. The pupils will be asked to draw maps and illustrations.
I will use a blackboard map and a 3D model, showing the river and bridge. Then I'll ask the children to name different parts of Coleraine and write them on their maps, and to say what they notice about the streets at the bridge (they all converge on the bridge). I'll then ask them questions about the lesson.

<u>Post-viewing impression</u>: I planned too much material. The lesson was a bit disorganized. They found the map hard to follow and the 3D model puzzled them at first. I could have saved time by doing all the labelling at once.

preparing specific lessons. For a topic or theme is a meaningful chunk in one's own head, but the individual lessons may not be so clear. Hence, there is much to be said in favour of preparing sets of lessons on a topic using mind maps, GAITO and, of course, key questions. Figures 6.3 and 6.4 give examples of student's lesson plans from a project with student teachers.

recording, identify what you think were the key questions in it. Listen for them and the children's answers. How accurate were you in your predictions? How could your use of key questions in that lesson have been improved?
3 Read and make notes on the two examples of a student teacher's attempts at lesson preparation given in Figures 6.3 and 6.4. What were the major

Figure 6.4   A student's second lesson planning record

Name: *V. Mitchell*   Topic area: *Journeys*   Class: *P5*   Date: *12/2/75*

Skill/s under review: *Reinforcement*   /G̶l̶o̶b̶a̶l̶   Time: *15 minutes*

Note on pupils' knowledge, if known: */*

1. Explicit objective/s   *By the end of the lesson the pupils will be able to solve simple problems based on journeys (or 'messages') in Coleraine. They will recognize that most journeys involve crossing the bridge and — I hope — they may suggest that Coleraine needs another bridge. (Mostly cognitive)*

2. Topic/method   *Mostly discussion, some discovery.*

   a) Introduction:

   Put up a large diagram of Coleraine. Ask children to show where they live, where the school is. Hand out diagrams on sheets.

   b) Development: *Tell them they have to explain to a visitor how to get from their school to different parts of the town. Ask each pupil a simple question. I'll start with P, he's still a wee bit shy so I'll give him an easy one. (Must remember to tell them to wait their turn and not shout answers out.) Praise each pupil. Then ask more difficult questions. If answers clear, tell them so. Then give them ten questions each involving messages (shopping, clinic, park, library, swimming pool, etc. All they have to do is to tick if they cross bridge, go through the Diamond, down Queen Street.*

   c) Completion: *Ask them for their answers. (I'll put questions on overhead projector whilst they're doing the problems.) Ask them if they notice anything about most of the journeys (messages). Ask them which way do cars passing through the town go to get to Limavady and Londonderry. Is this a busy bridge? What could the Council do to make it less busy?*

   d) Resources: *Diagrams, overhead projector, pens.*

   e) Pupil activities:

   Answer questions, discuss, follow map, solve problems.

3. Post-lesson impression

   Children enjoyed this. They wanted some more problems to do. Had to change question on the council to 'Should there be another bridge?' — of course they answered, Yes!

4. Post-viewing **impression**

   I used praise a lot and 'ah ha' too much. If anything, I over-reinforced and then couldn't get them to move on to the next part of the lesson. Must try to get the pupils to switch from one activity to another. G. suggested saying, 'That's been very interesting, let's move on now to the next bit because I think you'll find it interesting as well.' Children obviously enjoyed it. They kept opening their mouths to speak and interrupting each other, but they seem to understand the importance of taking turns. Making sure everybody got a chance to speak helped. Problem — can't see how that is possible in a large class.

Watching each other teach

differences between the first and second attempts? Compare your views with those of a colleague.

4 Think of a topic that you are going to teach. Spend ten minutes generating as many questions as you can about the topic. Sort the questions into groups and themes. Check that you generated a wide variety of levels and types of questions. What seem to be the key questions in this topic for a lesson with your class of pupils?

5 Think of a few questions on a topic, of the possible answers that individual children in your class might give and your responses to those answers. Then give the lesson and see to what extent you are accurate in predicting various individual children's responses.

6 Prepare a lesson using the ideas suggested in this Unit. Teach and audio-record the lesson. Invite a colleague to observe your lesson and to take notes on your use of questions and on the structure of the lesson. After discussion, listen to the audio-recording and identify the key questions and structure. Do the same for your colleague. Think of ways you might improve your questions. Reciprocal working of this kind can be very helpful for two teachers wanting to help each other to improve professional skills.

7 If you still have the audio-recording from your first lesson in this book, then listen to it again and consider in what ways you have improved your approach to questioning. Consider then how you might improve your questioning even further.

Good Luck!

APPENDIX: SUGGESTIONS FOR RUNNING WORKSHOPS

A workshop is a set of structured activities that provide opportunities for learning through thinking, practice and discussion. It is not a rambling seminar or an exploration of feelings – although discussions of feelings may occur.

To plan a workshop we suggest that you use the GAITO approach given in Unit 6. Begin with Goals and work through Activities for the participants, Inputs from the course tutor, Timing estimates for each segment of the workshop and the Order of events. Then check that the workshop that you have designed matches the goals. If it doesn't, then change the goals or the workshop. You should then consider how you are going to start the workshop and how you will draw together the themes at the end of the workshop.

The two final activities of the workshop should be the formulation of an action plan by each participant and a workshop evaluation. The action plan invites the participant to decide what he or she is going to do next – and when. The workshop evaluation is to obtain a measure of satisfaction of the participants and to improve the workshop. Questions on the workshop's interest, usefulness and intellectual challenge are useful. Open or semi-structured evaluations yield more insights, rating schedules yield apparently more precise measures.

Open-ended evaluations are more useful in the stages of developing a workshop.

A set of workshops could be based upon the Units of this text. Units 1 and 2 should be combined for this purpose. The Units could be tackled by the teachers in the school, with each teacher acting as facilitator and organizer for one Unit. Alternatively, teachers from neighbouring schools could come together for the workshop. This can be more fun.

The facilitator should prepare teaching inputs based upon the Unit and his or her experience of teaching and observing children. It is better to spend more time on a few of the activities than to attempt all of them in a short time. Examples of questions and responses of pupils and teachers that are drawn from your own classes and neighbourhood have a spontaneity and relevance that can rarely be matched by a textbook.

You could invite someone from outside the school or schools to act as a facilitator. Sometimes an external facilitator can bring a fresh approach to the topic, and he or she may stimulate colleagues to share views, experiences and enthusiasms that a familiar colleague may not or cannot do. But choose your facilitator carefully – particularly if this is the first time that you have provided such workshops.

ANNOTATED BIBLIOGRAPHY

Brown, G.A. (1978) *Microteaching: A Programme of Teaching Skills*, 2nd edn, London: Methuen.
One of the first texts in Britain to consider the component skills of teaching. Section Two contains suggestions and activities on explaining and questioning.

Dillon, J.J. (1988) *Questioning and Teaching: A Manual of Practice*, London: Croom Helm.
Dillon is probably the world authority on questioning. His text is replete with observations and suggestions.

Hargie, O. (ed.) (1986) *Handbook of Communication Skills*, London: Croom Helm.
Although not directly concerned with teaching, this text contains reviews of all the communication skills.

Kerry, T. (1981) *Effective Questioning*, London: Macmillan.
A guide for teachers in secondary schools, which contains useful hints and activities that may be modified for use with older primary school children.

Turney, C. *et al.* (1983) *Sydney Microskills Redeveloped*, Vols 1–4, Sydney: University of Sydney.
A most useful set of texts on the skills of teaching. Videotapes of relevant excerpts from lessons are also available from the School of Education, University of Sydney, NSW 2006, Australia.

Wragg, E.C. (ed.) (1984) *Classroom Teaching Skills*, London: Croom Helm.
A report and review of various studies of classroom teaching, including class control, explaining and questioning.

Wragg, E.C. (1993) *Primary Teaching Skills*, London: Routledge.
The report of the research findings of the Leverhulme Primary Project. Chapter 9 deals with research on questioning.

REFERENCES

Ausubel, D.P. (1978) *Educational Psychology: A Cognitive View*, New York: Holt, Rinehart and Winston.

Barnes D. (1969) 'Language in the secondary classroom', in Barnes, D., Britton, J. and Rosen, H. (eds) *Language, the Learner and School*, Harmondsworth: Penguin.

Barnes, D. (1976) *From Communication to the Curriculum*, Harmondsworth: Penguin.

Barnes, D. and Todd, F. (1977) *Communication and Learning in Small Groups*, London: Routledge and Kegan Paul.

Bennett, S.N. (1976) *Teaching Style and Pupil Progress*, London: Open Books.

Brown, G.A. (1978) *Microteaching: A Programme of Teaching Skills*, London: Methuen.

Brown, G.A. and Edmondson, R. (1984) 'Asking questions', in Wragg, E.C. (ed.) *Classroom Teaching Skills*, London: Croom Helm.

Clarke, C.M. and Petersen, P.L. (1986) 'Teachers' thought processes', in Wittrock, M. (ed.) *Handbook of Research on Teaching*, 3rd edn, New York: Macmillan.

Cockroft Report (1982) *Mathematics Counts*, London: HMSO.

Cox, C.B. (1989) *English for Ages 5 to 16*, the Cox Report, London: DES.

Delamont, S. (1984) *Interaction in the Classroom*, 2nd edn, London: Methuen.

Dillon, J.J. (1981) 'To question or not question in discussion', *Journal of Teacher Education* 32, 51–5.

Dillon, J.J. (1988) *Questioning and Teaching: A Manual of Practice*, London: Croom Helm.

Doyle, W. (1983) 'Academic work', *Review of Educational Research* 53, 159–99.

Doyle, W. (1986) Classroom organisation and management', in Wittrock, M. (ed.) *Handbook of Research on Teaching*, 3rd edn, New York: Macmillan.

Dunne, E. and Bennett, S.N. (1990) *Talking and Learning in Groups*, London: Macmillan.

Edwards, A.D. and Furlong, V.J. (1978) *The Language of Teaching*, London: Heinemann.

French, P. and Maclure, M. (1983) 'Teachers questions and pupil answers: an investigation of questions and answers in the infant classroom', in Stubbs, M. and Hillier. H., *Readings in Language, Schools and Classrooms*, 2nd edn, London: Methuen.

Gall, M.D. (1970) 'The use of questioning in teaching', *Review of Educational Research* 40, 707–21.

Galton, M. Simon, B. and Croll, P. (1980) *Inside the Primary Classroom*, London: Routledge and Kegan Paul.

Harrow, C. (1972) *A Taxonomy of the Psycho Motor Domain*, New York: Mckay Press.

Haynes, H.C. (1935) 'The relationship of teacher instruction, teacher exposition and type of school to types of question.' Unpublished doctoral dissertation. Baltimore, Md: Peabody College for Teachers.

Hergenhahn, B.R. (1988) *An Introduction to Theories of Learning*, New York: Prentice-Hall.

Mager, R.F. (1962) *Preparing Instructional Objectives*, Palo Alto: Fearon.

Mehan, H. (1978) 'Structuring school structures', *Harvard Educational Review* 48, 32–64.

Merlino, A. (1977) 'A comparison of the effectiveness of three levels of questioning on the outcomes of instruction in a college biology course', *Dissertation Abstracts International* 37, 5551-A.

Pate, R.T. and Bremer, N.H. (1967) 'Guiding learning through skilful questioning', *The Elementary School Journal* 67, 417–22.

Patrick, J. and Stammers, R. (1975) *The Psychology of Training*, London: Methuen.

Piaget, J. and Inhelder, B. (1969) *The Psychology of the Child*, London: Routledge and Kegan Paul.

Stevens, R. (1912) *The Question as a Measure of Efficiency in Instruction*, Teachers College Contribution to Education No. 48, New York: Teachers College Press.

Stodolsky, S.S., Ferguson, T.L. and Wimpelberg, K. (1981) 'The recitation persists; but what does it look like?' *Journal of Curriculum Studies* 13, 121–30.

Susskind, E. (1969) 'The role of question asking in the elementary classroom', in Kaplan, F. and Sarason, S. (eds) *The Psycho-educational Clinic*, New Haven: Yale.

Susskind, E. (1979) 'Encouraging teachers to encourage children's curiosity', *Journal of Clinical Child Psychology* 8, 101–6.

Taba, H. (1971) *Teaching Strategies and Cognitive Function in Elementary School Children*, San Francisco: San Francisco State College.

Tobin, K. (1987) 'The role of wait time in higher cognitive learning', *Review of Educational Research*, 57, 69–95.

Torrance, E.P. (1970) 'Freedom to manipulate objects and question asking performance of six year olds', *Young Children* 26, 93–7.

Turney, C. *et al.* (1973) *Sydney Microskills*, Sydney: University of Sydney.

Wragg, E.C. (ed.) (1984) *Classroom Teaching Skills*, London: Croom Helm.

Wragg, E.C. (1991) *The Leverhulme Primary Project*, Exeter: School of Education, University of Exeter.

Wragg, E.C. (1993) *Class Management*, London: Routledge.

Wragg, E.C. and Brown, G. (1993) *Explaining*, London: Routledge.

Wragg, E.C., Bennett, S.N. and Carré, C.G. (1989) 'Primary teachers and the National Curriculum', *Research Papers in Education* 4, 3.